DAYTONA 500

THIRD ANNUAL "DAYTONA 500"

and

NASCAR WINTER SAFETY AND PERFORMANCE TRIALS

1960 - 61 RACE SCHEDULE

DAYTONA INTERNATIONAL SPEEDWAY

DAYTONA BEACH, FLORIDA

OFFICIAL RACING GASOLINE

BE SURE WITH PURE

NASCAR SANCTIONED

DAYTONA 500

AN OFFICIAL HISTORY

BY BOB ZELLER

DESIGN BY TOM MORGAN

 DAVID BULL PUBLISHING

TABLE OF CONTENTS

Library of Congress Cataloging-in-Publication Data is
available.

ISBN 1-893618-19-6

David Bull Publishing, logo, and colophon are trade-
marks of David Bull Publishing, Inc.

Book and cover design:
Blue Design, Portland, Maine (www.bluedes.com)

Printed in Korea

10 9 8 7 6 5 4 3 2 1

David Bull Publishing
4250 East Camelback Road
Suite K150
Phoenix, AZ 85018

602-852-9500
602-852-9503 (fax)

www.bullpublishing.com

RIGHT: Thirty-seven cars race toward the first turn at
the start of the 100-mile qualifying race for hardtop
cars two days before the inaugural 500. Tim Flock
leads in a Thunderbird, with pole winner Fireball
Roberts to his left. Joe Weatherly is moving up on the
outside. The eventual winner, Bob Welborn, runs in
seventh on the inside lane.
PAGE 2: Three-color brochure of third annual Daytona
500.
PAGE 3: Lund celebrates his unlikely victory in 1963
with his wife, Ruth, and Miss Firebird, Linda Vaughn.
PAGE 4: Five years after his father, Lee, won the first
500, Richard Petty celebrates his first Daytona victory
in 1964 with visiting Japanese beauty queen Akiko
Kojima of Tokyo.

Preface

Every great sporting event is distinguished by its tradition, which is built by the unforgettable drama that occurs in the heat of battle, when the contest hangs in the balance.

The Daytona 500 began building its legacy with the very first running in 1959, when Lee Petty and Johnny Beauchamp roared side by side under the checkered flag. There has never been a closer finish.

But high drama has continued year after year as drivers and teams return to Daytona Beach every February to renew their quest to win NASCAR's biggest race. For a few, like Richard Petty and Cale Yarborough, success in the Daytona 500 came in abundance. For many, including Fireball Roberts, David Pearson, Buddy Baker, Darrell Waltrip, and, most notably, Dale Earnhardt, the Daytona 500 was more difficult to win than any other race, and they did not succeed until after they had lost more than they cared to remember.

Today, after more than four decades of races, the Daytona 500 is rich in its own lore. But the race was built on a motorsports tradition in Daytona Beach that dates to the birth of the automotive age at the beginning of the 20th century. The land speed record attempts of the early years gave way in 1936 to stock car racing on the beach, which continued until Daytona International Speedway opened in 1959.

The size and scope of the new 2.5-mile track was mind-numbing. NASCAR was only 12 years old when the speedway opened, and the largest track before then was South Carolina's Darlington Raceway, which was about half the size of Daytona. But it was those towering, high-banked Daytona turns that inspired the most awe. They allowed drivers to circle the track flat out. Lap speeds instantly were 25 miles per hour faster than they'd ever been. When Bill France built the speedway, he insisted the banked turns be flat to give the drivers the opportunity to race next to each other. France's prescience spawned a style of close-quarters racing that became synonymous with NASCAR.

Many of us grew up with the Daytona 500 on ABC's *Wide World of Sports* in the 1960s and remember twisting and turning the rabbit ears on our black-and-white television sets to improve the reception. In 1963, there was no instant replay to give us another look at that fast pit stop the Wood Brothers gave Tiny Lund before his improbable victory. But color television arrived in time to show us the Petty blue of Pete Hamilton's winged car in 1970, and instant replay was well established by 1976, so we could closely study what happened when Pearson and Richard Petty crashed on the last lap.

The massive track, the door-to-door action, the breathtaking slingshot passes, the close finishes— all of these ingredients not only helped make the Daytona 500 an instant success but also fueled its immense growth over the years. Between these pages are the stories and photographs of the men and machines who built the legacy of the Daytona 500 and made it the Great American Race.

ABOVE: A 1959 Pontiac Catalina speeds into the first turn during a quick lap around the oval in late 1958. Bill France Jr. was among the few who took fast laps on the lime rock base of the speedway just before it was paved.
OPPOSITE: Brightly painted sportsman race cars roar down the beach between a receding tide and a healthy crowd in this transparency from an early 1950s race on the beach-road course.

In the Beginning

The dawn of a new era in motorsports projected its first light in the form of a front-page article in the *Daytona Beach Evening News* on March 18, 1953.

"SEES POSSIBLE DOOM OF CAR RACING HERE" the headline blared.

The end of the beach-road races at Daytona Beach was in sight, NASCAR executive manager Pat Purcell told the city's Kiwanis Club on that Wednesday. Development doomed the beach-road course, he said. It was overcrowded, hard to manage, and always subject to the whims of the tides.

Perhaps the best solution, Purcell said, was to build an adequate speedway with proper seating and parking. "If something like this isn't done," he said, "it will very likely be done by some other community within a 100-mile radius of here. This isn't the time to talk. This is the time to do."

One month and three days earlier, 20,000 fans had packed the beach-road course at the end of Ponce Inlet for the 1953 Grand National stock car race. Some, no doubt, ignored the need for a ticket and bushwhacked their way to a viewing position, passing "Beware of Rattlesnakes" signs race promoter and NASCAR president Bill France had posted to discourage gate crashing.

The 1953 beach-road race was a wild affair. Fonty Flock snookered pole winner Bob Pronger into overshooting the first turn. Pronger flipped as Flock took the lead. The jovial middle brother of the racing Flock family led 38 of the race's 39 laps but ran out of gas on the final circuit and lost to Bill Blair, a little-known driver with only two previous Grand National victories.

The race showcased Detroit's finest 1953 models. Blair and Flock (who refueled and finished second) drove Oldsmobile Super 88s. Tommy Thompson was third in a Lincoln. Herb Thomas and Fonty's younger brother, Tim, finished fourth and fifth in brand-new models of the "Fabulous" Hudson Hornet.

A wide assortment of characters drove the 57 cars that took the flag on that blustery Sunday. Slick Smith finished 10th and behind him followed good old boys with names such as Buck, Red, Obie, Bub, Pop, Cotton, Hub, Lucky, and Perk. "Slow Poke" Travis finished 25th and earned $25, perhaps enough to get him home to Kentucky.

NASCAR's wild and woolly 1950s were at full steam in 1953. NASCAR itself was only five years old. But "Big" Bill France knew that racing on the beach-road course had to end.

"The beach course had been moved further and further south with the development of Daytona Beach," recalls William C. France, "Big" Bill's oldest son, known as Bill France Jr. "But even the south peninsula was starting to grow as we got into the 1950s. And the crowds grew. What never

OPPOSITE: On February 7, 1959, fans packed the grandstand to watch time trials—the first official event at Daytona International Speedway. Here, driver Gene White, the first qualifier, takes the green flag from Charles Moneypenny, the designer of the track, as Bill France looks at his watch.
BELOW: The original press and credentials office outside the speedway had a half-dozen walk-up windows next to a newspaper rack and a conveniently located phone booth.

changed was the amount of time you had between high tide and low tide. So as the crowds grew, it took longer to get them in and longer to get them off the beach."

The start of the 1952 race had to be delayed almost an hour while parking attendants sorted the challenges presented by an unexpectedly large crowd. The race was shortened from 48 to 37 laps, but some spectators' cars were swamped by high tide. The races caused monumental traffic jams, and area residents complained about the inconveniences. Crowd control was an even bigger problem. There were no barriers on A1A—the paved backstretch of the 4.1-mile course where the cars reached speeds of 150 miles per hour. By 1954, three new homes had been built in the middle of the course, their driveways feeding right onto the racetrack. "And you know," says Bill France Jr., "we were charging people for standing on somebody else's land."

On April 3, 1953, less than three weeks after Purcell had spoken to the Kiwanis Club, France arranged a meeting at Daytona Beach City Hall with city and county officials and the local legislative delegation. France was blunt. He was no longer interested in promoting races at the beach-road course. The headaches just weren't worth it. If Daytona was to retain its reputation as the speed capital of the world, it needed a million-dollar speedway. France proposed a banked racetrack of two or two-and-a-half miles that would be faster than the Indianapolis Motor Speedway and would accommodate crowds twice the size of those at the beach-road races. A single event could gross $300,000, perhaps $400,000, France said. He suggested a public-private partnership to build the track.

Everyone at the meeting agreed they didn't want the city's racing heritage to disappear. They agreed to work toward passing a local act that would create an agency to direct the construction of a speedway through the issuance of revenue bonds.

Racing had begun in 1903 at neighboring Ormond Beach, the "birthplace of speed." Ormond was the end of the train line at that time, and the wide, flat beaches at Ormond and Daytona were well suited to speed trials. Ransom E. Olds reached 50 mph in the "Pirate" and reported, "You have no idea what a thrill it is out there." By 1905, cars were topping 100 mph as land speed record attempts on the measured mile became an annual affair. Year after year, in dramas replete with triumph and tragedy, records were broken time and time again. In 1927, at Daytona Beach, Major Henry Segrave hit 203.97 mph. In 1935, driving "Bluebird," the most famous car ever to run on the beach, Sir Malcolm Campbell hit 330 mph on one pass. But this was also the last land speed run ever made at Daytona Beach. Later that year, Campbell moved to the Bonneville Salt Flats in Utah, which were smoother and wide open.

City officials and local racing enthusiasts sought a way to keep Daytona on the racing map. They organized a 250-mile race for stock cars on a combined beach-road course in March 1936 and offered a fat $5,000 purse that attracted some of the finest drivers in the country, including 1934 Indianapolis 500 winner "Wild" Bill Cummings. A huge crowd of at least 20,000 jammed the course, but the race was a fiasco. The sandy turns became so rutted, cars sometimes couldn't get through. The race was

BELOW: After the twin tubes were placed for the fourth-turn tunnel, Bill France inspected the progress. At left is Spike Briggs. Muse Womack is on the right.

BELOW RIGHT: The ground-breaking ceremony for Daytona International Speedway on February 13, 1958, did not prevent Bill France from actually getting started with the work. In this image, a marching band has taken its place for the ceremony as smoke rises behind them from burning stumps and cleared underbrush.

ABOVE: In the late 1960s, NASCAR President Bill France, who built Daytona International Speedway, stands in front of a photograph of the finish of the first Daytona 500 in 1959.

flagged early. Milt Marion was declared the winner, but it was impossible to conclude who really won. Bill France, who had moved to Daytona Beach in 1934, as a 23-year-old mechanic, was credited with fifth place. The city lost $22,000. Racing in Daytona was in grave trouble.

The next race was staged by the Elks Club on Labor Day in 1937. There was no purse to speak of. Nineteen of the 21 drivers were from Florida. Smokey Purser, a local rum runner, collected $43.56 for his victory. In 1938, France joined with Charlie Reese to promote two beach-road races. By then, France was one of the leading race car drivers in the Southeast. And he won the Labor Day race. As a promoter, he made his first profit, splitting $2,000 with Reese.

The fans returned as the races and the drivers became more competitive. By 1941, France was promoting four races—March 2, March 30, July 27, and August 24. World War II interrupted, but afterward, France continued the beach-road races and spearheaded the creation of NASCAR in late 1948. The first NASCAR Grand National (now Winston Cup) race was held in Charlotte on June 19, 1949.

When France proposed Daytona Beach's new speedway in April 1953, the most daunting challenge was that no one had any money to build it. Still, as France walked out of City Hall on that Good Friday after making his pitch to the local politicians, he was optimistic that within a couple of years, a new track would be built. He had no idea how long and hard he would have to work to make his dream come true.

At first, the path was smooth. On April 22, the City Commission of Daytona Beach formally asked the Florida legislature to create a special racing authority to oversee the project. In December, Lou Perini, the owner of the Milwaukee Braves baseball club, expressed interest in building the speedway. The estimated cost was $1,675,000.

Everything was going so well, France announced at 1954 Speedweeks that the beach-road course races that year would be the last. In 1955, the racing would be conducted on a spectacular new speedway, he said. Race fans wrote on their programs: "Last Race on the Beach."

On March 13, 1954, France rolled out the red carpet for Perini and his associates when they touched down in Perini's private DC-3. A marching band saluted the guests with song. Perini announced that he wanted nothing but the best. "I'm not just interested in another speedway," he said. He was ready to invest $3 million if need be.

In May 1954, France went to Indianapolis to explore promoting a NASCAR race at the Indiana state fairgrounds. The race never happened, but during his visit, on Thursday, May 13, France borrowed a guest pit badge from a man he knew who was an Indianapolis 500 lap sponsor. As France strolled through Gasoline Alley at the Brickyard, he was spotted by officials of the American Automobile Association, which sanctioned the Indianapolis 500. AAA, which was the nation's most powerful automobile racing sanctioning body, had been at odds with NASCAR since France started it. AAA officials notified chief steward Harry McQuinn. Minutes later, France was escorted out.

"It was an unfortunate thing," France told author Bill Neely in the late 1970s in *Daytona USA*. "It certainly wasn't [speedway owner] Tony Hulman. He and I were friends. It was the old AAA contest board, and they were jealous of NASCAR."

Did the insult strengthen his will to build the speedway?

"Well, it didn't hold us back any," France said.

Three weeks later, France received his first big setback on the speedway project. On June 4, Perini backed out. His engineers had advised him that the highways in the area couldn't handle the traffic that would be generated by the mammoth speedway he envisioned. Perini never broke ground in Daytona.

The legislature in the meantime approved the creation of the Daytona Beach Racing and Recreational Facilities Authority to assist in building the speedway. The five-member group was headed by J. Saxton Lloyd, a past president of the National Automobile Dealers Association and the owner of Daytona Motor Co., where France had once worked.

In the wake of Perini's withdrawal, the city and county directed the authority to explore the possibility of building a municipally owned speedway. And on August 27, the new authority members voted to accept a proposal from a Cincinnati bond house to sell revenue bonds to raise the money to build the track. The bonds would be backed by the revenue from speedway events.

By this time, it was obvious the speedway would not be completed by February 1955 as planned. France announced on September 14, 1954, that he would promote Speedweeks races on the beach-road course for just one more year in 1955. The beach-road course, as it turned out, hosted races for four more years.

In 1955, France created the Daytona Beach Motor Speedway and signed a 99-year lease with the authority to operate the yet-to-be-built speedway, which was to be located on a piece of municipal

OPPOSITE: Bill France and two associates examine the placement of the dirt for the banked turns in July 1958 during the early stages of the construction of the speedway.
LEFT: Bill France (right), Don Smith of Zink-Smith Company, and Bill France Jr., (left) study a map of the speedway in 1958 as ground clearing gets underway. Bill Jr., 25, was actively involved in clearing the land, which was completed by Smith and his company. Zink-Smith moved more than a million cubic yards of earth during the project.

land next to the city airport. Under the agreement, France paid $400,000 in advance rent. But authority members soon learned that they were outcasts by aligning themselves with France and NASCAR. The rival AAA issued a statement that it would refuse to sanction any speedway races on the track if France controlled it. *The Indianapolis Star* called the project a "pipe-dream speedway."

The authority kept pushing ahead, but other, more immediate problems slowed the project. The Civil Aeronautics Authority (forerunner of the Federal Aviation Administration) objected to the plans, mostly out of concern that the speedway would interfere with airport operations. Local political infighting also threatened to slow the process. Still, in June 1955, France predicted the speedway would be done by July 4, 1957, at an estimated cost of $2.5 million.

By November 1955, the county had begun expanding the local highways to handle the extra traffic that would be generated by the speedway. The CAA hurdles were cleared in December 1955. The authority on December 30 approved a bond issue for $2.9 million. But the procedural requirements needed to actually sell them ate up the first half of 1956. By the time the bonds hit the market in the fall of 1956, a recession was taking hold, money was tight, and interest rates were impossibly high. The baby boom era was in full bloom, and countless school bonds had flooded the market, along with the highway bonds that were financing the rapid growth of the country's highways.

"The timing wasn't very good," says France Jr., "and with the high interest rate that they were going to have to pay the bond holders, the event wouldn't support that kind of debt structure. It was going to be too expensive."

By April 1957, the authority had exhausted all its financing possibilities with revenue bonds. It began considering general obligation bonds, which are underwritten by tax dollars and must be approved by the voters. As plans were being made to put the measure on the ballot, taxpayer protest groups, full of retirees who had no interest in racing, began calling for a delay.

By May, it was obvious the measure wouldn't pass if placed on the ballot in 1957. In late summer, the referendum was postponed. Lloyd wrote that year: "Each problem was resolved only to find, frequently, that another problem had moved in to supplant the first. Delay after delay was imposed upon us through circumstances beyond [our] control." Lloyd spoke of the possibility of a pay-as-you-go construction program but warned that the speedway might take eight to 12 years to build. Thomas Cobb, the attorney for the speedway authority, said, "There is nothing wrong with the Daytona Beach Speedway project that a little cash won't cure."

On June 7, 1957, problems erupted on another front. The automobile manufacturers suddenly pulled out of the sport. Their move came several weeks after a crash at Virginia's Martinsville Speedway injured four spectators. It was a huge blow to NASCAR. France responded, "Business will continue as usual." That summer, as Lee Petty, Speedy Thompson, Marvin Panch, and Buck Baker won races with-

BELOW: Hometown hero Fireball Roberts powers through the north turn of the beach-road course in his No. M-1 1955 Buick on his way to an apparent victory in the 1955 Grand National race. Roberts' victory was disallowed when post-race inspectors discovered the push rods in his engine had been slightly altered.

JUNIOR JOHNSON
Ronda, N. C.

SHEP LANGDON
Durham, N. C.

G. C. SPENCER
Inman, S. C.

TOMMY IRWIN
Purcellville, Va.

RICHARD PETTY
Randleman, N. C.

FIREBALL ROBERTS
Daytona Beach, Fla.

BOB WELBORN
Greensboro, N. C.

JOE WEATHERLY
Norfolk, Va.

BOBBY JOHNS
Miami, Fla.

TINY LUND
Harlan, Iowa

LEFT: This stock car racing promotional brochure from 1960 reflects Bill France's understanding that the drivers were the stars of the show.

out factory support, France began devising the riskiest speedway plan of all: He would build it himself. He began talking with Lloyd, who was convinced that if anyone could do it, France was the man.

On October 24, 1957, the authority, now known as the speedway district, announced it had received a proposal from France to build the track. It set a November 8 deadline for the purchase of the now dormant revenue bond issue. When that day arrived and the bond issue died, Lloyd and France signed a fifty-year lease. The logjam had finally been broken.

The following day, France announced that his new company, the Daytona Beach International Speedway Corp., would begin building a 2.5-mile track at the airport site. Every grandstand seat would provide a view of the entire track, he said.

France's plans called for a low-budget $750,000 facility. He regretted he could afford no more. "Nobody feels worse than I do, and I have spent countless hours and considerable money during the past three years trying to fulfill that dream," he said. The first race—a 500-mile national championship late-model stock car race—would be in 475 days, on February 22, 1959.

On November 25, 1957, ground clearing began for Daytona Beach International Speedway. By the first week of January 1958, bulldozers had cleared almost a third of the area needed for the track. But it was slow going, and equipment often became stuck in the swampy portions of the land.

The final race on the beach was February 23, 1958. Paul Goldsmith led every lap, but Curtis Turner staged a classic charge in the closing laps, broadsliding into the sandy turns as only Turner could do. On lap 30 of 39, Turner took it in too hard and spun in the north turn. He recovered and mounted another charge but lost by just five car lengths. After 23 years of races, the beach-road course era was over. It had ended under a gray sky in chilly weather with a classic race.

Meanwhile, France's new company had gone public and was offering 300,000 shares of stock at $1 each. The stock sold in nine months, but money was being spent faster than it was coming in. Some of the speedway's strongest corporate partners have been there from the beginning because they were willing to take a risk when France needed them most.

"The Pure Oil Company and 76 fuel gave us some money back then to become the official fuel provider," France Jr. says. "They also gave us a $35,000 line of credit for fuel for the construction equipment." 76 fuel [now owned by Tosco Corp.] is still the official fuel of NASCAR and the speedway.

At one point, France needed $30,000 or the dirt movers would stop. He called a friend at Coca-Cola and said if he could come up with $30,000 in four or five days, France would publish a Coke ad in every NASCAR program for the next 10 years and give Coke product exclusivity at the speedway. Coke turned him down. France made a cold call to Pepsi, which immediately accepted the offer. Pepsi has been with the track ever since.

Paying bills was a week-to-week challenge in 1958. Construction began in April, and the costs quickly exceeded $750,000. Earthmovers removed dirt from the infield area to build the banked turns, creating a huge rectangular manmade lake along the backstretch. It was named Lake Lloyd.

France risked all he had, backing loans with his personal credit. He contacted a wealthy acquaintance, Texan Clint Murchison Jr., who referred him to his financial adviser, Howard Sluyter. France and Sluyter hit it off. Sluyter not only arranged for a $600,000 loan but also averted one financial crisis by writing a personal check to France for $20,000. "If it had not been for Clint Murchison and Howard Sluyter, we never would have accomplished the job of building the speedway as it is today," France said in *Daytona USA,* published in 1979.

France spent the $600,000 loan on grandstand seats (18,000 were built) and immediately began selling tickets. "And we used the ticket money for construction just as fast as it came in," France recalled. "We spent $2 million between the time the first tree was knocked down and we had the speedway completed. Which I didn't have the year before." Eventually, France paid off all his debts.

Engineer Charles Moneypenny was among those who worked on the project without immediate compensation. Moneypenny suggested a D-shaped track like the one he would design in 1967 to be Michigan International Speedway. France requested the tri-oval. Says Bill Jr., "He didn't want the drivers to have to be in a constant turn from the time they went into the third turn until the time they came out of the second."

A common misconception is that the banking was as steep as asphalt could be laid. "What controlled the steepness of the banking was the subgrade underneath the asphalt," Bill Jr. says. "When we piled dirt up there, we piled it to where you could compact the dirt and it wouldn't slide down the hill." The steepest it would stick was 31 degrees. This is what the banking became. Bill Jr. took some of the first laps around the track. He drove a passenger car on the white ribbon of hard-packed lime rock before the asphalt was laid.

Drivers often dropped by during construction. And as the track neared completion, their anticipation grew. As they drove through the tunnel and came up into the infield, they were greeted with a sight to behold. It was *big.* To their left was a massive banked turn that was so huge, they couldn't see all of it. To their right, another banked turn was so far away, they could hardly see it.

Mechanix Illustrated auto editor Tom McCahill stopped by for a visit in January. He wondered how slow a car could go without rolling off the banking. "You sure can't park there," he said. "It's no track for amateurs."

Jimmy Thompson took a look and said, "There have been other tracks that separated the men from the boys. This is the track that will separate the brave from the weak after the boys are gone."

By February 1, NASCAR's press agent, Houston Lawing, who was the speedway's new public relations director, was swamped with requests for stories and press passes. He wasn't sure how to accommodate all the requests for photographer credentials. "Some of those cameramen had better bring their long-range lenses," he quipped. "They may have to shoot from De Land" (21 miles west of Daytona).

At 2 p.m. that day, the track was opened for the first trial runs by race cars. Some of the guardrail remained to be installed. But it was almost done, so they went out. A crowd of 6,500 watched. One of the drivers was Turner, perhaps the greatest beach-road course driver of them all. Almost immediately, Turner did a lap at 143.1 mph in a Ford Thunderbird. Then hometown hero Edward Glenn "Fireball" Roberts was clocked at 145.7 mph. The lap speeds were as fast as the measured mile speeds the drivers were posting while driving flat out in a straight line on the beach! Fireball said, "The only limit on the speed is how fast the car will go and how fast you've got the nerve to drive it."

At one point, France wheeled a 1959 Pontiac Catalina pace car onto the track and turned a lap at 114 mph. The NASCAR president, long retired as a driver, had a lap speed that was nearly as fast as the fastest lap of the entire 1958 season, which was 116.952 mph by Eddie Pagan to win the Southern 500 pole at Darlington Raceway. Stock car racing was entering a whole new era, and the only thing Bill France didn't think to bring with him was a photo-finish camera.

OPPOSITE: After the lime-rock surface had been worked into the banked turns, but before the track was paved, Fireball Roberts posed with a race queen and a 1959 Pontiac Catalina, the passenger version of the car he drove in the first Daytona 500.

1959

THE FIRST RACE AT DAYTONA INTERNATIONAL SPEEDWAY was a 100-mile convertible race on February 20, 1959, two days before the first Daytona 500. The convertible race was immediately followed by a 100-mile race for the Grand National "hardtop" cars. Thus was born the concept of twin qualifying races to set the field for the 500—a tradition that continues today.

The first 500 was a "sweepstakes" race that included both hardtops and convertibles from NASCAR's convertible division. This was the only year convertibles competed in the 500. It quickly became apparent that they had a tremendous aerodynamic disadvantage. And it was not a comfortable ride, since the driver felt as if he were being sucked out of the car.

Among the competitors in the convertible race was a tall, skinny, jug-eared 21-year-old named Richard Petty. His father, Lee, the reigning NASCAR Grand National champion, was driving in the hardtop race. Richard had been racing less than a year, and he had started only nine Grand National races. Money was tight, so Richard was driving his well-used 1957 convertible. For the first time, it carried the number 43. (He had raced car number 2 in most of his 1958 events).

Petty was not intimidated by the speed, but the first laps seemed to take forever he said. "I thought I would never get back around," he recalled. During that first race, Petty and the other drivers discovered the profound aerodynamic effect the cars had on each other while running together at high speed. Petty quickly learned that he if tucked in close under the draft of the car just ahead, it broke the wind for him and allowed him to ease off the gas without losing any speed. Then, when he was ready, he could floor it and accelerate past the other car with a "slingshot" pass. "It was almost like finding extra horsepower," he said.

Right from the start at Daytona, fans saw the close-quarters style of racing that would set NASCAR apart from other motorsports. During the final nine laps of the first qualifying race, Glen Wood, Marvin Panch, Lloyd "Shorty" Rollins and Petty swapped the lead five times in their "ragtops." Wood was leading the last lap but wound up fourth. Petty decided to give the slingshot pass a try and blew past Rollins on the backstretch to take the lead. About the time Petty was congratulating himself, Rollins and Panch shot back by him. Rollins nipped Panch at the finish line by a few feet.

Thirty-eight hardtop cars lined up for the Grand National qualifying race. Bob Welborn, who had his greatest success in convertibles, led all but seven laps. But he could not shake the T-Bird driven by Fritz

Wilson, whom he would beat by only a half a car length. After the race, Welborn made some of the first recorded comments about the draft: "There I was, breaking the wind for him, and I couldn't seem to shake him. You know, when another car follows you real close, it causes a drag on your own car."

There were no accidents in either race. Rollins had averaged 129.5 mph in winning the convertible race, while Welborn had run his race at a staggering average speed of 143.19 mph. He had run 40 laps at a speed fast enough to qualify for the Indy 500.

It was too much for some drivers. Glen Wood didn't enjoy it, and he raced only in the first 500. Richard Petty had no problems with it, but his father wasn't entirely comfortable. "This track was really different, so big it made you wonder about things," Lee said. "I'll tell you what—there wasn't a man there who wasn't scared to death of the place. What it amounted to was that we were all rookies going 30 to 40 miles per hour faster than we had ever gone before."

Long before the green flag fell, however, Lee Petty had made a calculated decision. He knew the Daytona 500 would be the most demanding event he had ever driven in. Petty decided he needed a strong car, and he converted a big, sturdy 1959 Oldsmobile 88 into his race car.

Nearly all the 6,000 rooms in the Daytona Beach area were full by the night of the qualifying races. Travelers were referred to private homes, but new requests were still coming in by the minute on the day before the race.

A rainy race day would have been a crippling blow, considering Bill France's tenuous financial situation, but Sunday, February 22, 1959, was warm and sunny. The crowds poured into the new speedway. Infield admission was $4. By the time the green flag fell, 41,921 had paid their way in, according to the Daytona Beach *Morning Journal.* But the crowd was even larger than that. The paper reported that at least 500 fans simply crawled under the fence at a spot within sight of a ticket booth. There was room for only one at a time, so they lined up, sometimes 25 or 30 at a time, and waited their turn. Still, France grossed some $500,000 from the race. He immediately used all of the race-day income to pay bills.

Clint Murchison Jr., the speedway's largest creditor, drove the pace car. Starter Johnny Bruner Sr. waved the green flag from the apron at the start-finish line, stepping forward to the edge of the banking as 59 brightly colored convertibles and hardtops roared past him. The field stretched from one end of the tri-oval to the other.

Welborn, Tom Pistone, and Joe Weatherly traded the lead 10 times in the first 22 laps, but many fans kept their eyes on Fireball Roberts, who was charging through the field from his 46th starting spot, with Tim Flock and Jack Smith drafting behind him.

RIGHT: On Wednesday, February 25, three days after the race, the Hearst Metrotone News of the Week movie footage of the finish arrived in Daytona Beach. NASCAR officials Bill France (left) and Ed Otto prepare to watch the footage with Pure Oil Company's Dick Dolan (right). **BELOW:** This sequence of still photographs of the finish of the first Daytona 500 was made from Hearst Metrotone newsreel footage and sent via Airmail Special Delivery from New York to Daytona Beach two days after the race. The starter's stand appears as a white area below the scoring stand.

Some cars immediately began falling off the pace and dropping out. Fifteen cars were out by lap 56, including those driven by Fritz Wilson and Richard Petty, whose engine blew after only eight laps. Roberts barged past Weatherly to take the lead on lap 23 and began pulling away from the field. After leading 21 laps, Roberts suddenly fell off the pace. The local favorite parked his car on lap 57 with a broken fuel pump. Welborn's engine blew on lap 75. Turner, Flock, Smith, and Pistone were slowed when their tires began chunking, forcing them to make unscheduled pit stops.

As the race entered its final 125 miles, only Lee Petty and the relatively unknown Johnny Beauchamp remained on the lead lap. Beauchamp was an Iowa driver who competed in the Midwest-based IMCA stock car series. Petty managed to lead 21 straight laps, but on lap 183 Beauchamp charged past as the battle intensified. Petty retook the lead on lap 185. Beauchamp went in front on 188. Petty passed him back the next lap, and Beauchamp returned the favor on lap 190.

As the two drivers streaked around the track, Weatherly caught their draft. Although two laps down, Weatherly stuck to the leaders like glue. Beauchamp would complain after the race that Weatherly helped Petty and "gave me a real rough ride."

ABOVE: Joe Weatherly, in the upper lane, is almost two laps down as Lee Petty's Oldsmobile noses ahead of Johnny Beauchamp's T-Bird in the final second of the race.

Petty led laps 192 through 195. Beauchamp managed to retake the lead on lap 196. But Petty whipped his big Oldsmobile past Beauchamp's T-Bird and went back in front once again on lap 197. They had traded the lead a dozen times in 49 laps. As Bruner waved the white flag, Petty was a car length in front of Beauchamp.

Around the big speedway they went for the final time. And as the three cars came off the fourth turn, they spread out. Weatherly went high. Beauchamp went low. Petty was sandwiched in the middle. They were side by side by side as they came toward the line.

France stood below the flagstand behind the retaining fence, one yard shy of the finish line. He leaned forward on his left knee, bent his big frame down, and peered hard as the cars flashed past. "Beauchamp," France thought. But he couldn't be sure. He realized he was too close for a good view. The cars had passed in a blur. Bruner, however, agreed that Beauchamp had won. In the control tower, Bill France Jr. wasn't sure. Beauchamp was announced the winner over the public address system. The fans at the finish line howled and jeered in protest.

Bernard Kahn, sports editor of the Daytona Beach *News-Journal*, polled a dozen writers. All agreed that Petty was ahead by a couple of feet. Petty himself was confident he'd won. Both cars went to victory lane, but Beauchamp was the driver who was feted. His victory was unofficial, but Beauchamp said, "I figured I had him about like this," as he spread his hands 18 inches apart.

Speedway photographer T. Taylor Warren had snapped the finish from the grass in front of the pits. He rushed to the darkroom. Everyone was clamoring for pictures. Warren's classic photograph seemed to leave little doubt that Petty had won. In the image, the nose of Weatherly's lapped car is ahead of Petty's. On the bottom, Beauchamp trails Petty by about three feet. His bumper is even with the back of Petty's hood.

In the turmoil of the moment, Warren's photo was not conclusive enough. The cars were still shy of the finish line, and Warren's angle was from some feet ahead of the line. On the other hand, another image taken by a cameraman behind the line showed Petty's car ahead as well.

Beauchamp looked stolidly at the pictures and said, "I hit my brakes just as soon as I crossed the line." France was skeptical. The tide was beginning to turn in Petty's favor. The next day, France began trying to acquire newsreel footage. He announced, "There won't be another stock car race on that track until photo-finish equipment is installed."

Petty relaxed in Daytona Beach and opened the *Morning Journal* the day after the race. The front-page headline read, "Evidence Builds Up To Support Petty." Photos of the finish that were being made for an ad campaign also showed Petty's car ahead. An amateur photographer who stood almost directly in line with the checkered flag captured a picture on common 120 mm film that showed Petty's car almost on the lip of the line and clearly in front of Beauchamp's.

On Wednesday, Hearst Corp.'s *The News of the Day* newsreel footage arrived from New York. It was the clincher. Petty had won. Sixty-one hours after the race ended, he was declared the winner. Petty said, "Man, I'd never have believed it myself that there could be a 500-mile race like this one. It was close. Too close."

France was exhausted but not embarrassed. The controversy had given him three extra days of national media coverage. It had been a thrilling race—fast and safe. Petty had averaged 135.521 mph over 200 laps of green flag racing. Not a single car had crashed. And at the end, Bill France's dream speedway, which had been so tough to build, produced the closest finish he had ever seen in 30 years of racing.

1960

THE INAUGURAL DAYTONA 500 HAD BEEN an exceptionally clean race, right through the incredible finish. Not a single yellow flag flew. It was a different story in 1960.

The tone was set on the first lap of the first 100-mile qualifying race, when six cars tangled in turn two, spun off the banking, and slid down the backstretch grass. Tommy Irwin's 1959 T-bird hurtled nose first into Lake Lloyd. It was a brisk, chilly day. Irwin scrambled out and, still helmeted, had to swim hard through the choppy, windswept water to reach shore as his car bubbled and sank behind him.

The next day, 37 cars crashed on the first lap of the 250-mile modified/sportsman race. It was "the most spectacular accident in the history of automobile racing," sports editor Bernard Kahn wrote in the *News-Journal*. Eight drivers were hurt, four badly enough to be hospitalized. Among those involved were Ralph Earnhardt, Elmo Langley, Wally Dallenbach, Joe Lee Johnson, Wendell Scott, Tiny Lund and Ed Flemke.

Fireball Roberts set the pace in practice and became the favorite to win the 500. The 31-year-old hometown driver had earned his nickname as a hard-throwing baseball pitcher in high school in Daytona Beach. The nickname fit him just as well in stock car racing, particularly at the new speedway. However, Roberts was convinced he was jinxed when it came to winning his hometown classic.

He had been racing on the beach since 1947, but his only first-place finish, in 1955, had been nullified after postrace inspection. When the new track opened, Roberts took to the high speeds like a duck to water. He came up short in the inaugural 500 but broke through in July with a dazzling performance to win Daytona's inaugural Firecracker 250.

As Speedweeks got underway in 1960, Roberts picked up where he had left off. He blazed around the track to win the pole at an amazing 151.556 mph. It was faster than anyone had ever gone at the Indianapolis Motor Speedway, much to the delight of Bill France.

Fireball was driving a new 1960 Pontiac prepared by Smokey Yunick, a skilled and inventive Daytona Beach garage owner. Bobby Johns, a slender, dark-haired Miamian competing in only his 23rd Grand National race, also drove a Yunick-prepared car. Johns drove the 1959 Pontiac Roberts had driven to victory in the Firecracker 250. Jack Smith and Cotton Owens were top prospects as well in their new 1960 Pontiacs.

Before the race, no one had considered Junior Johnson a threat, not even Johnson himself. The

OPPOSITE: On Feb. 12, 1960, drivers and mechanics gathered among some of the cars outside the NASCAR trailer for the drivers meeting that preceded the twin 100-mile qualifying races. In the center are the fast Smokey Yunick Pontiacs driven by Fireball Roberts and Bobby Johns.
ABOVE: The grass infield of the tri-oval is strictly off-limits during today's racing, but in 1960, track announcers parked their station wagon there and climbed to the roof to announce preliminary events during Speedweeks.

Six of the 37 cars that crashed in the modified/ sportsman race the day before the Daytona 500 are shown in this image. Spectators were four- and five-deep along the fence during the cleanup after the crash—the biggest in speedway history.

28-year-old race car driver and moonshiner from Wilkes County, North Carolina, was a hard charger, but his year-old Chevrolet had been thrown together at the last minute. Only a week before the race, John Masoni, owner of the Daytona Beach Kennel Club, the greyhound racing track outside the first turn that predates the speedway, convinced veteran mechanic Ray Fox to build and enter a car, but only after offering to pay double the price Fox would normally charge. Fox telephoned Junior, whose racing career had been interrupted in 1957 by an 11-month term in the federal penitentiary for moonshining.

"I liked Ray, so I told him I'd come down and see what we could do," Junior said in his biography *Brave in Life* (David Bull Publishing, 1999). But the Pontiacs were much faster than the Chevys, especially Junior's older model. "I about decided that I was wastin' my time," Junior said. "I was ready to come home."

During practice, however, Junior got behind Owens' Pontiac and discovered that in the draft, he could keep up with Owens, even though his car wasn't as fast. Junior kept the news to himself. He finished fifth in the first qualifying race, which was won by Roberts, who led flag to flag. Jack Smith led every lap of the second race. Motoring across the line two laps down in the first event was David Pearson, a 25-year-old driver from Spartanburg, S.C., who was making his first Grand National start. Pearson finished 17th and qualified for his first 500.

Race day was brisk and sunny, and the confident Roberts led the first 19 laps. Johnson started ninth and began to draft the Pontiacs—even pitting when they did. When Roberts fell out with a broken engine after only 51 circuits, Junior stuck with the remaining Pontiacs and actually led 45 laps in the middle of the race.

Eleven mishaps plagued the event. Sgt. George Green of Johnson City, Tenn., who flew back from military duty in Germany to compete, gave the crowd a thrill on lap 87 when his car burst into flames in front of the main grandstands. The blazing car went 300 yards before Green got it stopped and bailed out.

On lap 126, Tommy Herbert's car spun off turn two, hit a backstretch gate opening, and disintegrated. The engine landed 50 feet ahead of the chassis. Pappy Crane tried in vain to avoid the flying wreckage and flipped down the backstretch, landing upside down. Only Herbert was seriously injured.

Richard Petty took the lead from Johnson on lap 135 during the caution period for Herbert's crash and led his first laps in the 500. Petty, who was still looking for his first Grand National victory, remained in front until his father, Lee, took over on lap 164 during another yellow flag. This one was caused by a three-car crash in front of the main grandstand.

On lap 170, Johns sailed past Lee Petty and put Yunick's remaining Pontiac in front. Johns settled into a smooth, fast rhythm. Johnson rode Johns' bumper but was fast enough only to follow. Johns was running, as he said afterward, "quiet and easy." Then came, as Johnson recalls, "one of the damnedest things I ever saw on a racetrack."

Johns' car was hit by a gust of wind as it came off turn two on lap 191. The air pressure popped the rear window out of his car and sent him into a spin. As Johnson swept past, Johns nearly ended up in Lake Lloyd. But he brought the car under control and quickly rejoined the race.

LEFT: Only seven days after agreeing to build a 1960 Chevrolet for the Daytona 500, mechanic Ray Fox sits with Junior Johnson atop the car in victory lane.
BELOW: Driver Tom Pistone was so unnerved by the prospect of hurtling into Lake Lloyd during a crash, he had an air tank installed in the well behind the front seat with a line attached to an emergency breathing device.

"I felt the rear window glass go after the crosswind lifted my car," Johns said afterward. "When I felt it spinning, I knew then either Petty or Johnson would pass me, but I wanted to get that Pontiac back out there on the track and win the race."

Johnson, however, was long gone. He took the checkered flag 23 seconds ahead of Johns. Behind them, Tom Pistone, who had led 26 laps, spun his car off the last turn of the last lap. He slid backward and slammed into two other abandoned race cars, demolishing all three vehicles and tearing out 15 feet of fence. Pistone was hospitalized with broken ribs and other injuries.

It had been a brutal race. Twenty-one cars crashed or burned. In victory lane, Johnson talked of several close calls. He had come perilously close to Lake Lloyd when he had had to drive onto the backstretch grass to avoid Herbert's crash. There was so much mayhem in the 500 that the next two races, both in Florida, had to be canceled so the teams could rebuild and regroup. The Grand National series finally resumed in Charlotte two weeks later. There, Richard Petty won his first race.

Johnson would continue to drive until 1966, but his triumph in the 1960 Daytona 500 was the biggest of his 50 Grand National race victories. "It still amazes me that we won," he says.

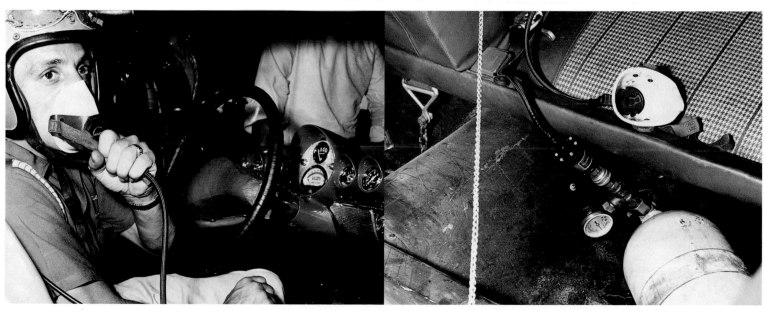

1961

FIREBALL ROBERTS WAS A MAN ON a mission as 1961 Speedweeks began. He was fastest from the start, setting new records in his stunning black-and-gold 1961 Smokey Yunick Pontiac.

Roberts won the pole position at a breathtaking 155.709 mph. Soft-spoken and articulate, the hometown native was the most popular driver in the sport. He even had a nightly Speedweeks program, *The Fireball Roberts Show,* on local station WNDB.

The blazing speeds matched the spirit of the nation. A young new president, John F. Kennedy, had committed the nation to the space race. Just down the road at Cape Canaveral, Alan Shepard was preparing for America's first manned space flight, which would occur on May 5. The link between speed and space exploration was underscored by the presence of an Atlas missile booster set up by the U.S. Air Force outside the fourth turn.

The question of the week was, "How fast can a stock car go?" At 155 mph, Roberts was 4 mph faster than 1960. Indianapolis cars would not reach 150 mph until 1962. But the risks became painfully apparent in the twin qualifying races two days before the 500.

As Roberts drove to victory in the first race, his march was slowed by five hair-raising crashes. Five drivers were hurt, though none seriously. The final crash came on lap 38 as Roberts and Junior Johnson battled door to door for the lead. The hard-charging Johnson ran over a piece of debris and lost control, clipping Richard Petty's Plymouth. Petty sailed over the guardrail in turn one. Johnson spun to a stop but was hit head-on by Jim Hendrickson. Johnson's steering wheel was pushed up to the front windshield. It took 15 stitches to close a cut on his chin—his only injury. Petty's car, meanwhile, somehow landed on its wheels outside the track. He suffered minor cuts and bruises but sprained his ankle getting out of the car. Petty limped to the edge of the high-

ABOVE: Not far from the track, a speedway sign advertises the upcoming month-long festival of speed at the new facility in 1961.

LEFT: Lee Petty cranks his steering wheel hard left in vain as he and Johnny Beauchamp sail out of the track and over the fourth-turn tunnel in their spectacular crash on the last lap of the second 100-mile qualifying race. Both drivers recovered from serious injuries.

OPPOSITE: Rescue workers work to free the injured Petty from the smoking hulk of his wrecked 1961 Pontiac. On the roof just above the passenger side window is the title, "The Blue Angels."

33

banked turn and waved as 17,500 fans cheered. By then, the race was over. Roberts was flagged the winner on lap 39—one lap short of the scheduled distance.

During the long intermission between the two races to clear the wreckage and fix the track damage, Lee Petty ventured out to see where his son had crashed. "It's hard to believe," he said. "What luck." The Pettys, in the spirit of the times, had nicknamed their race cars "The Blue Angels." Never would a nickname for two stock cars achieve greater irony. Less than two hours later, on the last lap of the second race, Lee Petty himself flew out of the track. But Lee was not as lucky as Richard.

As Joe Weatherly took the checkered flag to win the second race, Petty and Johnny Beauchamp entered the fourth turn battling for position, as they had in 1959. Both drivers were one lap down. Petty moved up to pass a slower car. His right rear touched Beauchamp's left front. Together, as if hooked, they shot straight up the bank and blew through the retaining fence, tearing out a dozen fence posts. They arced through the air toward the Atlas missile booster, then plunged over the embankment and tumbled to a stop just beyond the tunnel.

Petty was gravely injured. He suffered several fractures, a punctured lung, and internal injuries. At Halifax Hospital, as the story goes, he managed to tell France: "Bill, I want you to take Richard's driver's license away from him and get him a pilot's license."

France pointed out that Lee's car had probably gone 20 feet farther than his son's.

"Oh," Lee said. "Well, then maybe you'd better get me a pilot's license, too."

Lee Petty's career effectively ended with this crash, although he did return to race in six more Grand National races between 1962 and 1964. Beauchamp too suffered serious head injuries that curtailed his career.

The drama of the 100-milers set the stage for the largest crowd ever as 65,000 people jammed the track for the 500. Fifty-seven cars trailed Roberts into the first turn. Back in the pack, Bobby Allison, 22, and Buddy Baker, just 19, were making their first 500 starts.

Roberts led the first 12 laps, then traded the lead with Johnson, Matthews, and Nelson Stacy. Roberts began pulling away after he retook the lead on lap 43. By the late stages, Roberts was leading his teammate, Marvin Panch, by more than a lap. Yunick had tuned Fireball's car for high speeds but also to make the entire 500 miles on only three pit stops. Everyone else, including Panch, needed at least four stops.

Panch, 34, was driving Roberts' hand-me-down 1960 Pontiac. He had finished second to Weatherly in the second qualifying race. A Wisconsin native, Panch had begun driving on the West Coast in 1949 when the driver of a car Panch had built failed to show for a race. Panch drove the car himself and became hooked. By 1957, he was a NASCAR Grand National regular and had won six races. That year, he finished second in the championship to Buck Baker.

In the 1961 500, Panch was content to follow Roberts. "I tried to stay within sight of Fireball, which was pretty hard to do at times," Panch said afterward. "It was a fast race. I didn't expect to run that fast. I ran about 5 miles per hour faster all day than I wanted to. I'll tell you one thing, just keeping up with Fireball cut me out of drafting anybody else. I couldn't sit still long enough for that."

With 20 laps to go, Panch was in third, chasing Matthews. Two laps later, Matthews spun wildly in turn four when his engine blew. Panch took second and was happily contemplating a runner-up finish when, far ahead of him, the motor in Fireball's black-and-gold Pontiac began belching smoke. Thirteen laps remained. Roberts was through.

As Panch drove the final miles to the checkered flag, Roberts couldn't watch. He sat on a stack of tires in his nearly deserted pit, wearing a sweater over his driver's suit. Someone handed him a paper cup with water, but no one spoke to him. Finally, Yunick came up and put his arm around Fireball. When everyone was gone, Roberts finally rose to his feet, cursed, and hurled the smashed paper cup to the ground.

"I can't win here," he said, his voice choked with emotion. "I just can't win a big one here. The only big race I ever won in Daytona was on the beach and they took that one away from me. What the hell's with this place that I can't win here? The thing that gets me is that not once did I put my foot in it all the way around. It was just a nice, easy ride."

Panch finished 16 seconds ahead of Weatherly. Once again, the race had been run without a yellow flag. Panch averaged a blistering 149.601 mph, a world record for 500 miles. He had managed that speed despite four pit stops that totaled 3 minutes, 1 second. The soft-spoken Panch was well liked by his fellow drivers, but he was not a hell-raiser. He was a family man devoted to his wife, Betty, and their two children. He was nearly broke when he won the 500. He earned $21,000 for his victory, and the Panchs used the money to buy the Daytona home where they live today.

LEFT: After winning the race, Marvin Panch celebrates with his family and a swig of Pepsi in victory lane. Son Richie sits on the hood. Daughter Marvette is on the roof. His wife, Betty, stands by the car next to owner Smokey Yunick.

OPPOSITE: In this obscure photograph, a beefy Cale Yarborough, 22, wears his old high school football jersey and holds his helmet under his arm like a football as he poses for a publicity photo with his No. 52 1961 Ford for his first Daytona 500. Yarborough finished last, completing only four laps before the car's electrical system short-circuited.
LEFT: The infield lifestyle has always been an integral part of being a spectator at Daytona International Speedway. The state-of-the-art camper in 1962 included a lot of aluminum. Another breakthrough of modern living was the portable transistor radio. **BELOW:** Fireball Roberts poses in victory lane after his popular victory in the 1962 race. "I just didn't know if I would make it," he said afterward. His wife, Doris, tearfully said, "He has just driven his cotton pickin' heart out on this track trying to win the big one."

1962

BY 1962, FIREBALL ROBERTS WAS ENTRENCHED as the hard-luck king of his hometown track. He had been racing at Daytona for 15 years, and he had yet to win its biggest prize.

Roberts was disqualified after his only victory on the beach in 1955. He won the pole position for the first 500 and led 21 laps before dropping out with a broken fuel pump. In 1960, Roberts won his qualifying race and was the favorite to win the 500, but his engine blew on the 52nd lap. In 1961, he won the pole again and led his 40-lap qualifying race from flag to flag. And he ran away with the 500 until his engine blew with 13 laps to go.

The 1962 Speedweeks followed a familiar pattern. Fireball was the class of the field. He won the pole for his qualifying race in his Smokey Yunick-prepared 1962 Pontiac and again led from flag to flag, averaging 156.999 mph over the 40 laps to set an all-time Grand National race speed record.

For the top Indianapolis drivers, including the three previous winners of the Indianapolis 500—A. J. Foyt, Rodger Ward and Jim Rathmann—this was irresistible. They clamored to get the United States Auto Club (which had replaced the AAA as the nation's leading auto racing sanctioning body) to lift its ban on racing at Daytona. USAC, which sanctioned the Indy 500, would not budge. It wanted the drivers to focus on its own stock car racing series. The Indy drivers would have to wait another year.

The unpredictable action of Speedweeks, coupled with the high drama of Fireball Roberts' quest, made the race more popular than ever. Ten thousand new fans arrived, swelling the crowd to a record 75,000, according to media estimates. Roberts' wife, Doris, who was scoring for him, was caught in traffic and didn't reach the scorer's stand until lap 17. Someone else filled in until she arrived.

Before the race, Roberts ate his favorite food, a bologna and cheese sandwich. Then he went out and followed Yunick's instructions: "Drive her flat out—belly to the ground."

A furious battle erupted right from the green flag. Five different

RIGHT: This is what the inside of a stock car looked like two generations ago. On race day 1962, David Pearson crawled into this 1962 Pontiac Catalina built by Ray Fox and finished sixth, two laps down. It was Pearson's third 500.

BELOW: Tens of thousands of race fans filled out the order form printed on the other side of this ticket brochure to buy their tickets for the 1962 Daytona 500.

drivers traded the lead during the first 50 laps, including Joe Weatherly, who had won his qualifying race. Few if anyone paid attention when the No. 52 Ford dropped out of the race on lap four with electrical problems. Behind the wheel was 22-year-old Cale Yarborough of Timmonsville, S.C., destined to finish last in the 48-car field.

The pitched battle at the front saw Roberts lead the 15th lap, Cotton Owens lead on lap 16, Junior Johnson on lap 17 and Roberts again on lap 18. The blistering pace allowed the front-runners to lap nearly the entire field. But Yunick's flat-out strategy caused Roberts to run out of gas twice in the early going. During pit stops, Roberts rolled down his window by hand, just like a passenger car driver, to accept a drink.

Not far behind the front-runners was Richard Petty. He took the lead for the first time on lap 42. Petty was in a Plymouth that had started 10th, but his car was at least 10 mph slower than Roberts' Pontiac. Petty's team decided to try Junior Johnson's 1960 race-winning strategy and stay with Roberts at all costs—to draft him incessantly and pit when he did. Lee Petty, still limping from his devastating 1961 crash, stalked the pits during the final 125 miles, hands on hips, cigar in mouth, intently watching the battle on the track.

But this time, Fireball would not be denied. His nerves were frayed by the fear of yet another late-race calamity, but Roberts nonetheless turned laps at more than 155 mph in the late going and gradually distanced himself from Petty. Roberts won by 27 seconds. Petty finished second, the only other driver on the lead lap.

Roberts was giddy in victory lane. "I just didn't know if I would make it," he said. "I really sweated out those last 10 laps. It's like a dream come true. I'm just so happy I can't really believe it's happened."

Roberts said Petty never put any pressure on him. "In fact, I slowed down the last 50 miles," he said. Then he revealed that he had not precisely followed Yunick's directions. "The only time I went flat out was with Junior (in the early part of the race)," Roberts said. "From then on, I breathed the car in both turns. But I'll say this. That boy Richard Petty did a wonderful job of driving. He just drove the hell out of that car. He must have picked up about 5 miles per hour."

Petty, for the first time, had served notice that he would be a driver to reckon with at Daytona. With a wry grin, he told reporters, "I was just waitin' for (Roberts) to blow up." It didn't happen, and one of NASCAR's most popular drivers finally ended his jinx.

1963

ON FEBRUARY 14, 1963, 10 DAYS BEFORE THE 500, Marvin Panch, the surprise winner of the 1961 race, was at speed on the track in a Maserati, testing the sports car for the 250-mile American Challenge Cup race at Daytona two days later.

Panch had reached 163 mph in the modified, Ford-powered sedan, but as he eased off the throttle entering the third turn, the car went out of control. It slid to the apron, then began flipping. The Maserati cartwheeled up the track, hit the guardrail and came back down the banking. It finally slid to a stop on its roof, on fire.

First on the scene were two northern drivers, Bill Wimble and Ernie Gahan, who saw the crash as they came through the tunnel. Just behind Wimble and Gahan was driver DeWayne L. "Tiny" Lund, a 270-pound giant of a man, as well as two others. Panch was frantically trying to get out, but he couldn't get the door open.

The men tried to help Panch open the door, then started lifting the car to turn it over. Lund grabbed a fire extinguisher, stuck the nozzle through a tiny opening in the door and began spraying. Flames were erupting inside and outside the car. A gust of flame six feet tall drove the men back, burning two of them. They could see Panch still struggling, so they went back. This time, Lund helped lift the car. When they raised it 18 inches, Panch pushed the door partially open and stuck his legs out. Lund helped pull him out.

Panch was seriously burned. Gahan and two others also were burned. Months later, Lund and the four other rescuers were awarded Carnegie Medals for their heroism. But Lund received an even better reward right away. He was named to drive for Panch in the Wood Brothers Ford. From the hospital bed where he would spend the next three months, Panch agreed with the Woods: Lund was the best man to replace him.

Lund was a hulking, moon-faced, 26-year-old Iowa native who owned a fishing camp on Lake Moultrie in rural South Carolina. He looked more like a defensive lineman

ABOVE: As the shadows lengthen in the waning laps of the 1963 race, a pit crewman flashes the message to leader Fred Lorenzen on lap 184 that he is to pit in eight laps. Lorenzen pitted on lap 192 as Tiny Lund went on to victory. **BELOW:** Tiny Lund leads Ned Jarrett in the No. 11 Ford off turn two in the late stages of the 1963 Daytona 500. Jarrett led 26 laps during the second half of the race, including lap 192. But he had to pit for fuel on the next circuit, handing the lead to Lund for good.

than a racecar driver. He had played high school football and basketball in Iowa, but preferred racing motorcycles. He spent four years in the Air Force as a flight engineer, then began racing stock cars in 1956 in the NASCAR Grand National and IMCA series. He loved fishing, and once held a world record for fresh water striped bass after catching a 55-pounder near his camp.

By 1963, Lund had raced in 131 Grand National races. He had won five poles and finished second a couple of times, but he had never won a race. In the early '60s, he cut back on his Grand National racing. He came to Daytona in 1963 expecting only to work on someone's crew. Now he had one of the best rides in the garage.

Lund quietly secured the 12th starting spot for the 500 with an uneventful sixth-place finish in the second qualifying race, which was won by Junior Johnson. In the first race, a 24-year-old USAC driver named Johnny Rutherford electrified the Speedweeks crowd with his victory. The USAC drivers had finally convinced their sanctioning body to lift its ban on Daytona racing and they had come south in full force, including A. J. Foyt, Troy Ruttman, Jim Hurtubise, Parnelli Jones, Rodger Ward and young Rutherford, who had yet to race at Indy.

The Chevrolets had shown the most speed during the week, and Rutherford was driving a Smokey Yunick-prepared Chevy. Rutherford had blistered the field with a record qualifying speed of 165.183 mph. He battled with Rex White in the late stages of the qualifying race before taking the lead for good with five laps to go.

Race day was windy and wet. A squall blew through, delaying the start. It did not seem to dampen the excitement. For the first time, ABC's *Wide World of Sports* was covering the event. The popular Saturday afternoon show had debuted in 1961 with broadcasts of unusual and obscure sporting

OPPOSITE: The green flag falls at the start of the second 100-mile qualifying race in 1963 on a clear, chilly February 22. Pole winner Fred Lorenzen in the No. 28 Ford leads Tiny Lund in the No. 21 Ford. Johnny Rutherford came from the ninth starting spot (fifth car on the inside row) to win the race. **ABOVE:** Still giddy in the afterglow of his unlikely victory in the 500, Tiny Lund relives the events of the day. At far left, kneeling, is Steve Petrasek, a Firestone Tire representative, who helped Lund, save Marvin Panch from his burning sports car earlier in the month. Petrasek, Lund, and three others received Carnegie Medals for their actions.

41

events. Bill Flemming was the anchorman. In the pits, announcer and *National Speed Sport News* publisher Chris Economaki, dressed in a suit and wearing black-framed glasses, said, "Never before have we seen such tremendous enthusiasm for an automobile race."

The race delivered all the thrills anyone could have hoped for. Fireball Roberts had won the pole in a special 25-lap race, but his car was down on power. He led the first 10 laps of the 500 only because they were run under a yellow flag to help dry the track.

When the green flag came out, Junior Johnson and Paul Goldsmith darted ahead and were 30 car lengths in front during the early laps. But Johnson dropped out after 26 laps with distributor problems and Goldsmith was gone by lap 39 with a broken piston.

On lap 70, a handsome young Ford driver named Fred Lorenzen emerged as a force. G.C. Spencer and Foyt were battling side by side on the backstretch when Bobby Johns and Lorenzen darted to either side. Johns went high, Lorenzen went low and the cars were four wide. Lorenzen shot into the lead and stayed there for the next 35 laps.

But no driver could pull away. The lead pack always included five to seven cars. Shortly after

RIGHT: Tiny Lund, who filled in for injured Marvin Panch after helping save his life in a fiery accident, poses with car owner Glen Wood in front of the race-winning car. Lund drove the car in six other races that year and his finishes included a second, a third, a fourth, a fifth and a sixth.

halfway, Lorenzen began swapping the lead with Johns and Ned Jarrett. Lund was lurking in the background, plotting a different strategy. The Wood Brothers didn't even have the fastest Ford. But the high speeds were making engines gulp gasoline. It appeared that many cars would be unable to make it on the usual four pit stops. The Wood Brothers had vowed to do it, but they cut it close. Lund ran out of gas just before his third stop and coasted to the pits.

With 44 laps to go, Lorenzen pitted for the fourth time. His crew opened the hood and poured a can of oil into the engine. They filled the gas tank, but changed no tires. The stop took 38.1 seconds. Lorenzen wiped his own windshield as he left the pits.

Jarrett took the lead for two laps, then came in for a 36-second stop. On lap 158, Lund led for the first time when Jarrett pitted. With 40 laps to go, Tiny finally came down pit road. The Wood Brothers, displaying their pit-stop speed for the first time on national television, were done in a startling 26.9 seconds. Lund left the pits still in the lead.

As the afternoon shadows lengthened across the track, Lorenzen passed Lund and opened up a 20-car length lead. But by lap 185 Lund and Jarrett had caught back up. A furious battle ensued among the three drivers. Flemming leaned toward his microphone and said, "We've got a dandy going on here today at Daytona!"

On lap 192, Jarrett took the lead as Lorenzen peeled off the track and headed to the pits. He was out of gas. The next lap, Jarrett had to pit. Lund kept going. And going. He ran out of gas in the final turn, but when he coasted under the checkered flag, he was 24 seconds ahead of Lorenzen. Jarrett finished third, the only other driver on the lead lap.

In victory lane, the astounded young driver bellowed out a hog call, and told Economaki he'd be spending his winnings on his fish camp. Three weeks later, on March 16, the race was aired on *Wide World of Sports* (along with dog sled races from New Hampshire). For the first time, a national audience was exposed to the drama and excitement of the Daytona 500.

1964

BY 1964, RICHARD PETTY HAD ESTABLISHED HIMSELF as one of the most competitive young drivers in the NASCAR Grand National series. Still only 26, Petty was starting his fifth season. He had already won 28 races, including 14 in 1963, when he finished second in the championship to Joe Weatherly.

Petty was quickly becoming NASCAR's most popular driver, not only for his driving skill but for his congeniality. His father, Lee, was tough and irascible. Richard was friendly, outgoing and always happy to autograph a fan's program with his big, loopy, free-flowing signature.

All of Petty's 28 victories had come on short tracks. The Petty Engineering Plymouths had suffered from a lack of power on the superspeedways for several years, although Richard had skillfully driven to a third-place finish in the 1960 500 and had placed second to Fireball Roberts in 1962.

The 1963 race underscored the horsepower dilemma. Petty was the highest finisher who wasn't driving a Ford. But that was only good enough for sixth place, two laps down. As early as late 1962, racing insiders were speculating that Chrysler would upgrade its racing program.

By the end of 1963, Chrysler's new program was in full swing. It had produced a new, streamlined Plymouth. And it was testing, as secretly as possible, its powerful new "Hemi" engine at the Goodyear test track in San Angelo, Texas. Word leaked that the new car had reached an unheard-of lap speed of 180 mph.

After Daytona opened for practice, the rumors proved to be true. Petty and fellow Plymouth driver Paul Goldsmith easily surpassed 170 mph. Speeds were 15 mph faster than the previous year. "The feeling of the Hemi was unbelievable on the high banks," Petty said in his biography *King Richard I.* "The power was there all the time. It didn't matter when you punched it, it socked you right back in your seat. It sounded like it was going to suck the hood in."

The 426-cubic inch Hemi engine, which earned its nickname from its distinctive hemispherical combustion chamber, was a concept Chrysler had resurrected from its past. Hemi engines had powered the famous Kiekhaefer Chrysler 300s in mid-1950s NASCAR

43

OPPOSITE: At age 26, Richard Petty was emerging as one of NASCAR's brightest stars when this photograph was taken at Daytona before his first 500 victory. Petty had won 14 races in 1963 and would win eight more after Daytona as well as his first NASCAR Grand National championship.
RIGHT: With shadows lengthening across the track, Richard Petty makes a pit stop late in the 1964 Daytona 500. He led all but 16 laps. Chief engine builder Maurice Petty, sporting Petty blue footwear, helps change the treaded right front tire.

races. But the powerful engine proved impractical for most passenger car owners, and it was discontinued in an economy move in 1957. Chrysler brought the Hemi back into racing in 1964, but did not widely market the engine for production cars—a fact that proved more and more controversial as the year wore on.

But at Daytona, as the Plymouths blistered the track, the most common reaction was awe. Petty was more confident than he had ever been. For the first time, his car was as powerful as any other. Even so, the gains had not come easily. After first receiving the engine, the Pettys had discovered that the head gasket leaked. Chief engine builder Maurice Petty, Richard's brother, modified the engine to correct the problem.

Junior Johnson was a happy convert to the Hemi as well. He was driving a Dodge. He used to call them "goats" because they were so slow. Not anymore. Johnson pulled a slingshot pass on Buck Baker's Petty Engineering Plymouth in the final turn of the first 100-mile qualifying race and won by a car length.

In the second race, Petty ran away from the field. But on the last lap, as he cruised a half lap ahead, the big Hemi engine burned its last drops of gasoline and went dead. Behind Petty, Bobby Isaac and Jimmy Pardue came roaring toward the finish line side by side. All three cars seemed to cross the finish line at the same moment, Petty coasting at 40 mph. It was three hours before the photo-finish picture proved that Isaac had beat Pardue by a foot.

The 500, however, was all Petty's. Paul Goldsmith led the first lap, but Petty was passing him as they crossed the line to start lap two. Isaac and A. J. Foyt also mounted early challenges and led a few laps. But Petty retook the lead on lap 52, passing Goldsmith on the high side of turn four, and led the rest of the way.

He won the race in style, rim-riding at 175 mph just a few feet from the outside wall. He had started using the upper groove during his first practice in 1959. It allowed him to get better runs off the turns in his underpowered cars. Now, with all the power he would ever need, Petty used the upper groove to even greater advantage. He made the victory look easy, but said afterward, "I wasn't exactly enjoying myself out there. You've got to stay right with the car every second at the speeds we're going now."

Petty later said that the only unfortunate aspect of his first 500 victory was that his wife, Lynda, was not there to see it. Their children, Kyle and Sharon, had the measles. Lynda, pregnant with her third child, remained at the motel, nursing her sick youngsters as she listened to the race on the radio.

1965

NASCAR INSTITUTED NEW RULES IN OCTOBER 1964 to enhance safety and decrease speeds in 1965. The 1964 season had been marred by the deaths of Fireball Roberts and Joe Weatherly. And Ford officials were howling about the Chrysler Hemi engine, which had powered Richard Petty to blazing speeds on his way to victory lane in the 500. Petty had won eight more races in 1964 and his first NASCAR championship.

Ford wanted a new engine with high-rise cylinder heads to compete with the Hemi and threatened to pull out if Bill France didn't allow it. NASCAR's new rules, however, banned both Hemi engines and high-rise cylinder heads.

Chrysler competition director Ronney Householder announced that Chrysler was withdrawing from NASCAR unless France suspended the ban on the Hemi and gave the company a year to change to new equipment. Neither side backed down through the winter. And when 1965 Speedweeks started, the Plymouths and Dodges, as well as their drivers, were nowhere to be seen.

Paul Goldsmith returned to the USAC stock car series, which allowed Hemis. David Pearson and Bobby Isaac went to USAC as well. Petty said USAC didn't pay enough. He took an ill-fated turn into drag racing. Rising stars LeeRoy Yarbrough and Earl Balmer scrounged rides where they could. Jim Paschal went home to his chicken farm.

From this void rose Fred Lorenzen, one of the brightest NASCAR stars of the 1960s. Lorenzen was the "golden boy," a young, handsome, blond-haired Yankee who brought a new look to a garage full of good old boys. He was from Elmhurst, Ill., and had won his first racing purse—$100—in a demolition derby at Soldier Field in Chicago. He started racing modified stock cars there and in 1956, at 22, ran in seven NASCAR races without notable success.

Lorenzen began competing in the USAC series in 1957, and the next year won five races. In 1960, he returned to NASCAR and finished eighth in his first 500. In 1961, Lorenzen finished fourth in an underpowered Ford owned by Tubby Gonzales. That performance earned him a ride with the vaunted Holman-Moody Ford factory team.

In May 1961, Lorenzen outdueled Curtis Turner in a fender-banging battle at Darlington to win the Rebel 300. The shootout was televised on *Wide World of Sports* and made him a racing celebrity. In the next four seasons, Lorenzen won 19 NASCAR races, including the World 600 and three

straight Atlanta 500s, beating such notables as Roberts and Junior Johnson. By 1965, Lorenzen had become NASCAR's most glamorous star, with a reputation for winning the big ones.

Although the Chrysler teams were absent, there was plenty of competition among the Ford and Mercury drivers. Lorenzen, with his Holman-Moody Ford, was automatically one of the top contenders. But the weeks before the race had been anything but placid in the Holman-Moody garage. Just before leaving for Daytona, one of their young engine builders, Waddell Wilson, worked straight through the night one night to replace faulty cam bearings.

Darel Dieringer won the pole at a speed of 171.151 mph in Bud Moore's 1964 Mercury, then held off Ned Jarrett's move in the final turn to win the first 100-mile qualifying race. The second race became a duel between Lorenzen and Johnson. Lorenzen took the lead on lap 39. But when he roared under the white flag, he mistook it for the checkered flag. Lorenzen let off and Johnson passed him on the last lap to win. "I've got nobody to blame but myself," Lorenzen said.

The Chrysler pullout had attracted a wide range of independent drivers to Daytona, seeking to fill the gap. This contributed to a fiery, 13-car wreck on the first lap of the second qualifying race, as well as to a remarkable attrition rate in the 500 itself. By lap six, 14 cars were already out of the race, all because of mechanical problems.

Johnson grabbed the lead on the first lap from his second starting spot and led the first 27 circuits. He was racing in his usual go-for-broke style when a tire blew. Johnson's car hurtled into the outside wall and spread debris over a wide area. Johnson suffered only a cut over his eye. After Johnson's abrupt departure, Marvin Panch led through lap 68 in the Wood Brothers Ford, with Lorenzen and Bobby Johns on his tail. Lorenzen led laps 69 through 78 before giving way to Panch.

At halfway, Panch was still in control, but clouds were darkening over the track. On lap 119, Lorenzen edged past Panch and took the lead for only the second time. Rain was falling by lap 129. As the yellow light came on, Panch made a run on Lorenzen coming off turn two. Panch went to the outside, Lorenzen moved up, the cars touched and Panch spun down the backstretch, ending his chances for a second 500 victory.

Lorenzen remained in the lead, but the fender that had hit Panch's car was bent in on his tire. "Stay out," ordered crew chief Herb Nab, who was counting on the weather to shorten the race. Soon, it was pouring. The race was stopped after 133 laps and declared official. The Golden Boy had won NASCAR's biggest race. In victory lane, a wet but happy Lorenzen said, "I just never thought I could do it. This is the one I always wanted all my life." Of the incident with Panch, he said, "It seems like he tried to go between the fence and me. There wasn't quite enough room."

Panch was not particularly upset. "There's nothing real serious about it," he told Dan Gurney, who was working with the ABC *Wide World of Sports* team. "I don't think Freddy knew I was in there. The hole closed up and I kinda hit him."

OPPOSITE: Ron Eulenfeld triggered this wild crash coming out of turn four on the first lap of the second 100-mile qualifying race in 1965. Eulenfeld walked away from the fiery aftermath of the collision, which knocked 13 cars out of the race.

BELOW: With their rear ends hanging out, four cars speed through turn four early in the 1965 Daytona 500. Leading this pack is Junior Johnson in the No. 27 Ford, followed by eventual race winner Fred Lorenzen in another Ford, Earl Balmer in Bud Moore's 1964 Mercury, and Marvin Panch in the Wood Brothers Ford.

OPPOSITE: Pole winner Richard Petty and Dick Hutcherson are side by side as they lead a 50-car field under the green flag to start the 1966 Daytona 500. Petty went on to win; Hutcherson retired after 38 laps with a broken windshield.
LEFT: Driver Don White (left) sits on the hood of his 1965 red-and-white No. 07 Dodge with Sam McQuagg, while Larry Frank leans on the car on pit road during 1966 Speedweeks. McQuagg finished fifth, Frank was 10th and White was 27th after dropping out on lap 115 with ignition failure.
BELOW: Richard Petty holds the winner's trophy in victory lane as interviewers stand ready with their microphones. To Petty's left is Chris Economaki, a pit reporter for ABC's *Wide World of Sports.*

1966

THE DODGE AND PLYMOUTH TEAMS WERE BACK AT DAYTONA in full force for 1966 Speedweeks. The factory teams returned to NASCAR racing in mid-1965 after Bill France relaxed the ban on Hemi engines and allowed their use with certain limitations.

For Daytona, the Hemi engine was limited to 405 cubic inches of displacement and had to be used with the heavier Plymouth Fury or Dodge Polara models. These restrictions did not deter Richard Petty, who started right where he'd left off in 1964.

Petty won the pole at a record speed of 175.165 mph in his Plymouth. In the first qualifying race, however, Paul Goldsmith made a slingshot pass of Petty in the final 100 yards to win. It was Goldsmith's first victory since 1958, when he won the final race on the old beach-road course. The magic of another Daytona-style finish prevailed in the second qualifying race as well. Earl Balmer passed Dick Hutcherson on the final lap. In that race, a young Italian immigrant and Indy-car driver named Mario Andretti led a single lap before falling back.

Curt Gowdy, a baseball and football announcer, anchored his first Daytona 500 in 1966 for ABC's *Wide World of Sports.* "This event is only eight years old, but. . . has grown so much in stature, that today the largest sports crowd in the history of the South may be here to watch the world's fastest cars and top drivers," Gowdy told his audience. "This is my first trip to Daytona and I've been amazed at the magnitude of this event and the feeling of anticipation and excitement."

Two-time Indy 500 winner Rodger Ward, a color commentator, described trying to drive at 175 mph: "You can drive in there without even lifting the throttle. It's very difficult to do at these speeds, but you can."

All the cars had a noticeable drift in the turns. They ran with their back ends hung out. And in the race itself, the tires proved no match for the blazing speeds. Petty and Goldsmith traded the lead during the first 18 laps, lapping slower cars within a few laps of the start. But Petty suddenly veered off and headed to the pits for an unscheduled stop. His left front tire was blistered. He lost a lap.

Pieces of rubber began littering the track, and chunks of tread smashed the windshields of three contenders, including Dick Hutcherson and Wood Brothers drivers Marvin Panch and Curtis Turner. All three had to drop out.

Jim Hurtubise had one of the fastest cars but made several extra pit stops because of flat tires. He eventually finished sixth. As far as Turner was concerned, Hurtubise caused problems for others with his disintegrating tires. "He's already knocked three Fords out—Hutcherson's, Panch's and mine," Turner told ABC pit reporter Chris Economaki.

Petty, meanwhile, was slowly climbing back toward the leaders. But another unscheduled stop set him back. The *Wide World of Sports* audience watched one of those pit stops as Maurice Petty shook the tire to get

it off the wheel, then secured the new tire by picking up the lug nuts off the ground and putting them on the studs by hand. It took the jack man 10 to 15 pumps to jack the car, and Richard himself reached out to clean his own windshield.

Petty was two laps down at one point, but he drove "harder than I think I ever had" to get back to the front. On lap 97, he passed Goldsmith to retake the lead. Petty took the lead for good on lap 113, passing Cale Yarborough, who led the race for the first time. Yarborough, in his fifth 500, took the lead three times for a total of 33 laps. As Petty took over, Goldsmith was no longer a threat. He had chunked a tire and his drive shaft was warped. He came to the garage. It took his crew 15 laps to fix the car.

As the race entered its final laps, Petty was rim-riding in the high groove, building a lead that eventually grew to more than a lap. The clouds began to thicken and a few drops of rain sprinkled onto the track. Then it began to rain harder. The yellow flag flew. The race was called on lap 198 with Petty a full lap ahead of Yarborough. David Pearson was third, another lap down, and Fred Lorenzen finished fourth.

Petty's average of 160.627 mph was a record, even though he needed seven pit stops. Petty was the first driver to win the 500 more than once. This time his wife was on hand to witness the victory, but it was not under the best of circumstances. Lynda Petty was drenched by the downpour that ended the race.

OPPOSITE: With new hardware for his trophy case, Petty poses in victory lane at the front of his Plymouth Belvedere. Petty went on to win six more races in the 1966 season and finished third in the NASCAR championship behind David Pearson and James Hylton.

RIGHT: Helmet in one hand, drink in another, Marvin Panch confers with Leonard Wood in the pits during 1966 Speedweeks as an *ABC Wide World of Sports* cameraman captures the scene. Panch's 500 ended after 119 laps with a broken windshield.

BELOW: These fans were among the first with motor homes in the Daytona infield when they came for the 1996 race. A 1950s municipal bus converted into a camper was the hot ticket back then, with plenty of room on the rooftop observation deck.

1967

WHEN CURTIS TURNER ARRIVED FOR 1967 SPEEDWEEKS AT DAYTONA, he was a full-fledged old-timer making a comeback in the twilight of his career. Turner was driving for Smokey Yunick, who had slipped out of stock car racing in 1964 after being a dominant force in the first five 500s.

Yunick returned in 1966 with rookie Mario Andretti, who had electrified Indianapolis in 1965 by finishing third in his first 500. Andretti was less fortunate in his 1966 Daytona debut. He crashed on the 31st lap.

In 1967, Yunick prepared a black-and-gold Chevrolet Chevelle for Turner. NASCAR rules allowed teams to cut back the fenders to accommodate the larger racing tires now being used. Yunick, ever the iconoclast, kept his fenders intact, realizing that the smaller openings would provide better aerodynamics, even if the wheels rubbed a bit.

In practice, Turner blew through the 180 mph barrier and reached 181.5 mph on the day before qualifications. He won the pole with a track record of 180.831 mph. Turner was the only driver to qualify above 180 mph. Yunick promptly cut the fenders back after qualifications, and spread the word that he wasn't using his best engine.

If anyone was underpowered, it was Andretti, who had returned to Daytona in 1967 as the second driver for Holman-Moody, driving a Bill Stroppe Ford. John Holman didn't want Andretti. Holman and many others thought Andretti was too short to drive a stock car. But Ralph Moody had taken Andretti under his wing, even if it meant major modifications to the driver's compartment. "The chair is like a baby chair," Moody said. "He's so short, the pedal and throttle had to be built up."

Andretti was slower than most until crew chief Jake Elder admitted to him that Holman had given him engines with medium risers instead of the high risers that teammate Fred

Lorenzen's car had. Andretti went to Holman, who brushed him off. Andretti then complained directly to Jacque Passino, Ford's motorsports chief. Within days, Andretti had the new, more powerful engine.

Although he was on Firestone tires, which were slower than the Goodyear tires in 1967, Andretti reached 180 mph with the new powerplant. When he tried the Goodyears just to see what he could do, he ran 181.5.

Andretti didn't break 180 mph in qualifications, but he led nearly half of his 100-mile qualifying race before fading to sixth. Like many others, Andretti had to stop for a quick splash of fuel to finish. Lorenzen ran easy, drafted other cars and won on a single tank of gas. The first race was won by LeeRoy Yarbrough, a 28-year-old short-track demon from South Carolina who had finished eighth in the 1966 500. Yarbrough passed A. J. Foyt with five laps to go and held on for the victory. Foyt complained that he was blocked by Tiny Lund on the final lap. Foyt was so mad, he briefly threatened to pull out of the 500.

If the qualifying races suggested anything, it was that the competition was close. Besides Yarbrough and Foyt, David Pearson and Paul Goldsmith had led laps in the first race, and Buddy Baker was strong as well. (Turner had quit after one lap, saving his car for the 500). In the second race, Lorenzen, Richard Petty, Cale Yarborough, Darel Dieringer and Dick Hutcherson had all run strong.

The action in the eighth annual 500 was as hot as the day was cold. A crowd estimated by the media of more than 94,000 fans jammed the track as Turner led a 50-car field to the green flag. Turner led the first lap, but Yarbrough passed the old veteran to lead the second and third laps. Then Foyt took over. Seven drivers led during the first 50 laps, including Andretti, Baker and Pearson. The leaders passed and repassed each other almost at will.

ABOVE: Mario Andretti drives the Holman-Moody Ford into the gray stuff at the upper edge of turn four as he races with Jerry Grant during the 1967 event. In the lower groove cruises Henley Gray, seemingly on a Sunday afternoon drive with his hand out of the window. Gray was running 27 laps down at the finish.

A series of minor spins and crashes slowed the fearsome pace, which nonetheless began to take its toll. Yarborough damaged his suspension avoiding a crash on lap 42. Two laps later, Foyt's clutch failed. Two laps after that, Hutcherson crashed. Yarbrough was next, gone on lap 71 with engine failure.

All the while, Andretti thrilled the crowd with his let-it-all-hang-out style of driving. His car was set up loose, which is the way he wanted it. Andretti had requested the softest anti-roll bar possible for his car. Andretti was fastest with his loose car when he dove to the edge of the apron entering the turns, then let the car drift all the way to the wall, its back end hanging out almost like a sprint car on dirt. Twice a lap, he would drift clear across the banked turns without losing pace. For the fans, it was thrilling to watch. For the other drivers it was unnerving. Most were certain he would never last 200 laps. Andretti's style also made him tough to draft with.

The fierce battle continued at the front, with Baker, Dieringer, Pearson and Andretti trading the lead. Lorenzen now emerged as a contender, taking the lead for the first time on lap 115. Five laps later, Baker's engine blew. Turner dropped out after 143 laps with the same problem. And on lap 159, while leading the race, Pearson blew his engine, causing another yellow flag.

Andretti led Lorenzen as they came to the pits for their final stops. They were the only drivers on the lead lap. Andretti became suspicious, then angry, when his jack man held his car in the air until Lorenzen's car cleared the pits. Lorenzen now led, but Andretti stalked him before the restart and shot into the lead as they drove under the green flag.

Tiny Lund, running a lap down in third, made a bid to unlap himself. Lund went side by side with Andretti, but couldn't get by. Andretti managed to break free, but Lorenzen couldn't get past Lund. By the time Lorenzen shook Lund, Andretti was 11 seconds ahead. Lorenzen couldn't catch up. In fact, he lost more ground. Andretti was flying, gaining a half-second, sometimes a full second, every lap.

On lap 198, when a yellow flag flew for Petty's blown engine, Andretti was 22 seconds ahead. He said afterward, "I was worried about Freddie. His car is the same as mine. But Freddy got to fooling around with Tiny and I just slipped away from them."

The tiny Italian, two days shy of his 27th birthday, had proved he could manhandle a big American stock car better than most drivers. Andretti went on to become one of racing's legendary drivers, winning the Indy 500 in 1969 and the Formula One World Driving Championship in 1978.

He said of his Daytona victory: "I was never in a race where there was so much jockeying around by the drivers. You have to go all over the track—high and low—and sometimes there's just a foot between cars. You don't baby a car at Daytona as you would at Indy. It's flat out and draft as much as possible."

1968

IN 1967, ONLY A FEW DRIVERS HAD CRACKED the 180 mph barrier. In 1968, it was no holds barred. LeeRoy Yarbrough caused the first stir on the opening day of practice with a lap of 184.432 mph in the Mercury owned by Junior Johnson, who had retired as a driver in 1966. Then Tiny Lund cracked 185, reaching 185.754 mph in Bud Moore's Mercury. Moments later, Cale Yarborough posted 185.758 mph.

The next day, Richard Petty mashed the pedal to the floor in his new Plymouth and ran 186.5 mph. Petty's car sported a black vinyl top, prompting much speculation about what advantage a trick roof might provide. (It provided nothing but trouble). Not long after Petty's run, David Pearson erased all previous marks with one lap of 188.2, followed by an astounding 190.746 mph. By the end of the day, Lund and defending champion Mario Andretti were in the high 187s.

Wrote *Charlotte Observer* motorsports writer Bob Moore: "In two days, a new era was started. An era that no one was prepared for." Yarborough described the sensations at 185 mph: "I can feel the G forces stretching the skin of my face. It seems like my arms weigh about 100 pounds apiece and my head about 200 pounds." At age 28, Yarborough had been racing in NASCAR Grand National events for more than a decade, but was only now beginning to come of age. The short, stocky, all-state high school football star from Timmonsville, S.C., had struggled for years, despite his natural talent and aggressiveness.

In 1965, he became an example of the "agony of defeat" on *Wide World of Sports* when he drove his Ford over the first-turn fence at Darlington and flew out of the track in the Southern 500. The footage became an instant classic. Yarborough walked away unhurt, with his sense of humor intact, and gained thousands of new fans. He won his first Grand National race that year.

In 1966, the Wood Brothers hired Yarborough to drive their No. 21 Mercury and he finished a distant second to Petty in the Daytona 500. In 1967, Yarborough won at Atlanta. And when Fred Lorenzen, the great Ford hero, retired in April, Yarborough filled the gap, winning the Firecracker 400 in July.

After the final flag flew in a windy afternoon of time trials on February 11, Yarborough was on the pole at 189.222 mph. Only the wind gusts, which reached 35 mph and caused drivers to lift in the

third and fourth turns, prevented Yarborough from circling the track at 190 mph.

The qualifying races were increased from 100 to 125 miles, but race day for the new Twin 125s dawned gray and wet. During a lull in the bad weather, Bill France told the drivers to buckle up. Many refused, arguing that the track was still too wet. Soon, more rain came and drowned the argument as well as the races.

Without the benefit of the qualifying races to test the draft at the higher speeds, drivers were more tense than usual before the 500. "It's pretty wild, I'll guarantee you that," Bobby Allison said, moving his hand as if to imitate a wiggling snake. Andretti said: "The cars are just too unstable when you get over 187."

Many drivers considered Andretti to be one of the main hazards, although he led three times for 17 laps during the first half of the 500. After Andretti crashed on lap 105 and took Buddy Baker and John Sears with him, one driver said, "He's the hairiest driver I've ever seen."

The race was filled with crashes. The yellow flag flew 11 times for 60 laps—both records. The pace car had to be on the track so often, one vehicle overheated, then another.

Yarborough had led the first 12 laps, but was forced to make two unscheduled pit stops between laps 13 and 16. His engine was skipping. When Leonard Wood jumped inside the car to replace the ignition, Yarborough yelled, "Man, you gotta fix this thing! It'll fly!" Wood replaced the faulty part and said, "Go get 'em, boy." Yarborough lost a lap, but with yellow flags flying so frequently, he quickly made it up.

On lap 62, Yarborough headed to the pits for another unscheduled stop. There was a hole in his right front tire. He lost another lap, but quickly made that one up, too. On lap 89, he took the lead

BELOW: By 1968, the Wood Brothers were widely considered the fastest pit crew in NASCAR. Here, the crew gives Yarborough's Mercury Cyclone a fast stop. Kenneth Martin holds the gas can. Glen Wood is at the windshield. Ralph Edwards has the air gun and Delano Wood runs with the jack.

for the first time and remained there for 55 laps until trouble struck again.

On lap 143, Yarborough peeled off the track yet again as Yarbrough took the lead. Now Cale's engine was running hot. Trash was jammed between the grille and radiator. Glen Wood cut a hole in the grille and yanked the trash free. Yarborough said afterward, "I was beginning to think this just wasn't supposed to be my day."

When Yarborough got back up to speed, he was three quarters of a lap behind LeeRoy Yarbrough. On lap 166, Yarborough made his regular pit stop, took gas only and headed back out. Two laps later, Yarbrough came back in. A *Wide World of Sports* camera captured the chaos in his pit as they waved him back out. Yarborough thought his crew had signaled him in. They hadn't.

Now Yarborough was back in front with a comfortable lead, but with one more regular pit stop to make. Another yellow flag flew and Yarborough pitted on lap 176, relinquishing the lead to Yarbrough. When the race restarted on lap 178, Yarborough was fourth, trailing Paul Goldsmith, Bobby Allison and Yarbrough. But his car was as fast as it had been all day.

Yarborough passed Goldsmith on lap 181 and Allison on lap 183. Now the battle was down to the two Mercury Cyclones, although Yarborough was still nine seconds back. Relentlessly, Yarborough narrowed the gap. By lap 189, he trailed by only three seconds.

As Cale closed in on LeeRoy, he thought he had plenty of time. But he couldn't see the scoreboard because his windshield was smeared with oil. Cale later said, "I thought there were about 15 laps to go. And then I noticed out of the corner of my eye a sign from Glen that there were only six laps left."

He made his first charge on lap 194, pulling even with Yarbrough on the backstretch. But he hit a patch of oil and had to back off. The next lap, Yarborough again pulled even with Yarbrough on the backstretch. This time, Henley Gray's lapped car was in the way. He had to back off again.

On lap 196, Yarborough made his third attempt. Again, he pulled even on the backstretch. This time, he shot ahead as they entered the third turn. Immediately, Yarborough began pulling away. When the checkered flag fell, he was 1.3 seconds ahead of Yarbrough. Allison was third, 25 seconds behind.

Not long after the race was over, Yarborough's mother began asking, "Cale, when are we going to leave?" He put her off at first, but she was persistent. Finally Cale agreed to leave, although he would have stayed and savored the victory longer if it had been up to him.

Cale was piloting his own Beechcraft Bonanza, and when they came within sight of the little grass airstrip in Timmonsville, the Yarboroughs could see cars parked everywhere. After they landed, someone rolled a red carpet up to the plane's door. The Timmonsville High School band marched out from behind a hangar, playing the school song. The mayor was there, holding a wreath of roses. Yarborough had tears in his eyes as he walked down the red carpet.

"That's the reason Mama was so insistent that we leave," Yarborough wrote in his autobiography, *Cale*. "All those people had been waiting hours for me."

BELOW: During the pace laps before the start of the race, the 50-car field stretches from turn two almost to the start-finish line. The fifth row is the closest in this view, with Paul Goldsmith in the No. 99 Plymouth and Al Unser, who drove the No. 6 Dodge to a fourth place finish.

1969

WHEN THE SPEEDWAY OPENED FOR POLE QUALIFICATIONS on February 9, 1969, only seven cars went on the track. Never had Speedweeks been so quiet. The entire Ford contingent was waiting in the wings while the manufacturer tried to get a new 429-cubic inch "semi-hemi" engine approved by the Automobile Competition Committee of the United States (ACCUS), which supervised racing in the U.S. Only one Ford, LeeRoy Yarbrough's, was even at the track. All of Ford's top drivers were absent, including defending champion Cale Yarborough, David Pearson, new convert Richard Petty, Donnie Allison and A. J. Foyt.

That left the pole wide open for the Dodge teams, and Buddy Baker won it after fighting off the effects of a gust of wind that nearly put him into the second-turn wall. Baker's lap of 188.901 mph was just off Yarborough's 1968 record.

Two days later, ACCUS ruled that Ford could not use the engine at Daytona because it had failed to install the required number of 500 engines in production cars. Ford had rushed to produce 500 engines, but had failed to get them installed in cars. To the great relief of the speedway and NASCAR, Ford decided that it would enter its teams in the 500 anyway with the 427 c.i. engines they had used in 1968.

But another rules change limited teams to one carburetor. In 1968 they had been allowed to use two. Ford loyalists predicted the Dodges would blow them away. However, during a qualification run the day before the Twin 125s, David Pearson erased any notion that the Fords were underpowered. He broke the 190 mph barrier in his Wood Brothers Ford, setting a track record of 190.029 mph.

Pearson said, "Sure, we're giving away probably 75 horsepower to the Dodges, but the [Torino] body design is better aerodynamically, so that makes up the difference." The next day, Pearson captured the first 125-mile race and set another track record, reaching 190.274 mph on the 18th lap of the 40-lap event. Bobby Isaac, driving a Dodge, won the second race.

Hard luck continued to plague Yarbrough, as it had throughout the 1968 season. He had given away the 1968 Daytona 500, finishing second to Yarborough when he mistakenly thought he was being called into the pits and made an unnecessary stop. Yarbrough had gone on to lose other races he dominated that season, and to finish second in two more big events. He did manage to win two races.

Before the 500, Yarbrough blew an engine during practice, spun and smacked the wall. Car owner Junior Johnson was forced to pull out a back-up car. Then, on lap 36 of the first Twin 125,

ABOVE: In the days before live telecasts of the Daytona 500, some fans took advantage of the opportunity to watch the race live on closed-circuit television at movie theaters around the South. This brochure advertised telecasts in Noth Carolina.

63

Yarbrough's rear window popped out, sending him into a spin. He didn't hit anything, but had to pit for new tires. He finished ninth.

Yarbrough's luck began to change the day before the 500. He won the Permatex 300 race for late-model sportsman cars. Driver Don MacTavish lost his life in a savage crash, and the garage was sad and tense on the morning of the 500.

Fans packed the grandstands and infield. For the first time, media estimates put the crowd at more than 100,000. They witnessed a safe race, with only a few relatively minor incidents. The worst scare came when defending champion Yarborough lost a tire and slammed the fourth turn wall. Yarborough was carried to an ambulance, but suffered only cuts and bruises.

Baker, in the pole-winning Dodge, and Donnie Allison, a Ford driver, dominated the first half of the race. Charlie Glotzbach, driving the Cotton Owens 1969 Dodge, took the lead on lap 119 and led the next 20 laps before giving way to Allison.

On lap 161, Yarbrough passed Allison and took the lead for the first time. Allison fell back and it became a shootout between Yarbrough and Glotzbach, the only drivers who remained on the lead lap throughout the race. On lap 178, Glotzbach whipped his Dodge past Yarbrough and took the lead again.

When Yarbrough came to the pits for his final stop on lap 181, crew chief Herb Nab replaced the left rear tire with one made of a softer compound. Nab knew it would grip better. He just hoped it wouldn't wear out in less than 20 laps. Yarbrough emerged from the pits nearly a full lap behind Glotzbach.

Five laps later, Glotzbach made his final stop. Back at speed on the track, Glotzbach still led, but now Yarbrough was only six seconds behind. Fourteen laps remained. With the softer tire, Yarbrough was cutting Glotzbach's margin by more than a half second a lap.

Yarbrough's relentless charge brought the speedway's largest crowd to its feet. Closer and closer he came. With three laps to go, the gap was one second—just 275 feet. A last-lap showdown seemed inevitable. Yarbrough kept coming. On the final lap, he went high in turns one and two to get a run off the corner. As the two cars shot down the backstretch for the final time, Yarbrough squeezed up close to Glotzbach's bumper and pulled out to pass.

Glotzbach recalled later: "I just didn't know anything to do."

They went side by side into turn three, but as the cars came out of turn four, Yarbrough had the lead. He passed under the checkered flag with Glotzbach glued to his bumper.

Overcome by emotion, Yarbrough and his crew cried tears of joy in victory lane. They had finally broken their jinx. Yarbrough said, "I just can't find words to express how exciting this is."

But it was only the beginning. Yarbrough went on to have one of the finest seasons in NASCAR history. He won seven times and nearly swept the major races, with victories in the Rebel 400 and Southern 500 at Darlington, the World 600 at Charlotte, the Firecracker 400 at Daytona, the Dixie 500 at Atlanta and the American 500 at Rockingham.

OPPOSITE: LeeRoy Yarbrough celebrates with a Union 76 race queen after his emotional victory. "The tires made the difference," Yarbrough said. "I was thinking I might run second again but I saw I was gaining on him. I knew the car had the power when I needed it."
BELOW: On the last lap, these two cars battled in the race's final showdown. Yarbrough, driving Junior Johnson's No. 98 Ford, made a slingshot pass of Charlie Glotzbach on the backstretch and won by a car length.

1970

ABOVE: The towering wings of
two Dodge Daytonas—the
essence of a brief but
memorable era in stock-car
racing—loom over pit road
during 1970 Speedweeks.
The wings were built tall so
the trunk would open.

BELOW: The Petty Enterprises
crew services Pete Hamilton's
SuperBird during the race.
Hamilton won in part because
of the extra grip he had when
the team changed two tires
during the final round of pit
stops, then called him back in
to change the other two tires.

THE 1969 NASCAR GRAND NATIONAL SEASON had been marked by the opening of Talladega and the boycott of the inaugural Talladega 500 by most of the regular drivers, who complained that the track was unsafe. Bill France ran the race anyway and the controversy slowly disappeared. By 1970 Speedweeks, pure speed was once again the only concern.

Cale Yarborough returned with the Wood Brothers after spending the winter recovering rather than relaxing. On December 7, in the final race of the 1969 season, the inaugural Texas 500 at Texas International Speedway, Yarborough blew a tire on lap 143 and slammed the outside wall. He shattered his shoulder blade. Some feared his career was over. "When this bone is broken this badly, usually the patient is dead," one doctor said.

Recovery was supposed to take six to nine months, but Yarborough was ready to go by Speedweeks. He took two slow laps in the first practice, then ran 188 mph. After practice, Yarborough said he wasn't even sore. And when he won the pole at 194.015 mph, his record-setting lap was the talk of the garage for the rest of the week. It was more than 3 miles per hour faster than the previous mark, 190.706 mph, which he had set in July 1969.

Two days after streaking to the pole, Yarborough walked away from "a very near thing" when the nose wheel of his twin-engine Piper Aztec collapsed as he was beginning a takeoff run at his hometown airport in Timmonsville, S.C. The plane skidded to a stop on its nose.

But neither broken bones nor close calls kept Yarborough from charging to victory in the first Twin 125 qualifying race a week later. Yarborough dueled with Bobby Isaac before both made pit stops on lap 32. Yarborough took fuel only and was gone in 15 seconds. Isaac stayed for new right-side tires and came back on the track about 12 seconds behind Yarborough. At the end, Isaac was still five seconds behind. Finishing fifth in the first race was Pete Hamilton, a blond-haired Massachusetts driver who had distinguished himself as the 1968 Grand

National rookie of the year and earned the ride in the second Petty Enterprises Plymouth SuperBird—the famous winged car.

The second Twin 125 was won by Charlie Glotzbach, who was also recovering from injuries. Glotzbach had been shot and wounded less than three months earlier by a disgruntled employee. Glotzbach was content to follow Buddy Baker for a time, but swept past Baker on the backstretch on lap 37 and slowly padded his lead, winning by 4.7 seconds. The race was marred by the death of Talmadge Prince in a first-turn crash. It was Prince's first Grand National start.

Fate played a major role in the 500, claiming one driver after another almost as soon as the green flag fell. Richard Petty was the first victim. His SuperBird engine blew after only seven laps. Petty retired and went to the Hamilton pit to help direct operations there. Yarborough led 26 of the first 31 laps and was pulling away on lap 32 when his engine suddenly blew as he passed the main grandstand.

The Ford teams seemed particularly prone to trouble. Nine laps after Yarborough's departure, Donnie Allison's engine expired. A. J. Foyt's engine failed on lap 58. Defending champion LeeRoy Yarbrough came to the pits on lap 75 with ignition trouble in his Ford. He lost seven laps.

It became a race between Glotzbach and Isaac, with Hamilton lurking in the shadows. The sole remaining hope for Ford was Holman-Moody driver David Pearson, who had started 31st (Pearson had dropped out of his qualifying race after shredding a tire). Pearson took the lead for the first time on lap 68 and battled with Isaac for 15 laps until a cut tire put Isaac a lap down.

Glotzbach was in front at the halfway point, but gave way to Pearson on lap 118. After a series of green flag pit stops, Pearson was about eight seconds ahead of Hamilton and 12 seconds ahead of Glotzbach with 57 laps to go. On lap 158, Glotzbach passed Hamilton. Glotzbach was only about four seconds behind Pearson when he pitted on lap 167. But Glotzbach left without his gas cap and was called back in, ending his chances.

Now only Pearson and Hamilton remained on the lead lap, and Pearson was firmly in command. Once again, fate stepped in. Dick Brooks blew an engine and spun on lap 187, bringing out a yellow flag. Both Pearson and Hamilton pitted. Pearson took two left-side tires and Hamilton took two

OPPOSITE: Pete Hamilton
celebrates in victory lane with
a bevy of beauty queens.
Hamilton started only 64 races
in his brief NASCAR Grand
National (now Winston Cup)
career, which lasted from 1968
through 1973. But he won four
races—both events at Talladega
in 1970 and a Twin 125 in 1971.
RIGHT: Dick Trickle, a
Midwestern short track ace,
made his first NASCAR start in
1970 in the Daytona 500 at age
28. Trickle's engine blew a head
gasket and he retired after 131
laps. He finished 26th.
BELOW: Speeding through the
second turn, Bobby Isaac leads
Charlie Glotzbach in a pair of
1969 Dodge Daytonas. After
switching to a 1970 model in
May, Isaac won 11 races and the
Grand National Championship.

right-side tires. Since Pearson was still leading,
Hamilton's crew chief, Maurice Petty, knew he
had nothing to lose by having Hamilton pit again
for fresh left-side tires.

"Come in next lap and we'll change the left
sides!" Richard shouted to Hamilton during the first
stop. The two extra tires proved to be the difference.

The green flag flew again on lap 190. Two laps later,
Hamilton dove inside Pearson as they entered turn three.
They battled side by side all the way into the first turn
before Hamilton finally edged ahead. Hamilton had led
four laps earlier in the race, but that was while other leaders were pitting. Now he had passed his way into the lead.

As the largest crowd in the track's history, an
estimated 103,800 fans, stood on their seats,
Pearson looked for a way to get back around the
young SuperBird driver. On lap 198, Pearson
pulled alongside Hamilton as they sped into the
third turn. Side by side, they blazed around the
banking. But in turn four, Pearson's car slipped.
The back end bobbled. Both cars got out of
shape, but Hamilton recovered faster and shot out to a lead of five car lengths.

As the last lap started, Pearson was again on Hamilton's bumper. But Hamilton blocked Pearson
in the first turn, fended him off on the backstretch and was leading by three car lengths as they took
the checkered flag.

"I felt I could run fast enough to keep Pearson from slingshotting me if I could get in front,"
Hamilton said afterward. "We had planned to take it easy the first half of the race. I think we ran
quite a bit faster the last half. We could run with everybody." Said Pearson, "We probably should
have changed all four tires on that last stop."

Hamilton's 500 victory was the start of a successful year with the Pettys. He won both races at
Talladega in 1970 and posted 10 top-five and 12 top-10 finishes in 16 starts. Hamilton's NASCAR
driving career was over by 1974, but he had won stock car racing's most important race in one of the
most distinctive cars ever to run at the speedway.

1971

THREE MONTHS BEFORE 1971 SPEEDWEEKS, the landscape of the NASCAR Grand National series changed dramatically. During a tumultuous two-week period in late 1970, Ford Motor Co. pulled out of racing after a change in corporate attitude. At almost the same time, the R. J. Reynolds Tobacco Co. joined NASCAR.

Ford's announcement had come on the heels of a similar move by Chrysler, which cut its factory commitment from six teams to two for 1971. Ford's withdrawal clouded the future of some of NASCAR's most prominent car owners, including Holman-Moody, the Wood Brothers, Junior Johnson and Banjo Matthews. Jacque Passino, Ford's racing chief, quit the company. Cale Yarborough decided he'd seen enough and jumped into Indy cars, although he would run in the 500 in a Ray Fox-prepared Plymouth.

Without sponsorship, Ford owners Johnson and Matthews scaled back and prepared to drop out of the series, which they did later in the season. The Wood Brothers and Holman-Moody decided to press on without factory backing. An era was ending. Automobile manufacturers would never again dominate as the primary financial backers of NASCAR teams.

Fred Lorenzen, who came out of a two-year retirement in 1970, arrived at Daytona in 1971 driving a Plymouth prominently emblazoned with STP Oil Treatment decals on its quarter panels. Other companies, including Purolator, Dow Chemical and K&K Insurance, were already in the sport. Within a few years, stock cars were advertising many different products.

There were changes in the schedule, too, as well as in the rules. The stock car racing part of Speedweeks was shortened from 2 1/2 to 1 1/2 weeks. And in August 1970, NASCAR ordered carburetor restrictor plates for the first time. Speeds had escalated beyond the tolerances of tires. Three drivers—Bobby Allison, Bobby Isaac and David Pearson—were the first to suggest the plates, which reduced speeds by restricting the amount of fuel and air that could pass through the carburetor. But the plates immediately ignited controversy because the differences in engines prompted NASCAR to mandate a different-size plate for each car maker.

The plates reduced practice speeds by about 15 miles per hour. A. J. Foyt's pole-winning speed of 182.744 mph was more than 11 mph slower than 1970. Still, Foyt was significantly faster than everyone else, all of whom were below 180 except Bobby Isaac, who reached 180.050 mph.

Richard Petty and Buddy Baker, driving the only factory-backed entries in the race, were third and fourth fastest in qualifications. Petty was driving a new Plymouth Road Runner. Baker, who replaced Pete Hamilton in the second Petty Enterprises entry, was driving a Dodge. If the Petty cars had an advantage, it wasn't apparent. A dozen drivers were practicing at about the same speed.

In the first Twin 125, as the field thundered through the last lap, Foyt was in command. Suddenly, ahead of him in the fourth turn, a lapped car driven by Ron Keselowski spun, hit the wall and flipped. Foyt cracked his throttle. Hamilton, trailing Foyt, kept his foot on the gas. Hamilton pulled alongside Foyt and beat him by approximately three feet.

In the second race, David Pearson won after apparently using a "cheater" restrictor plate in his Holman-Moody 1969 Mercury. Two days later, NASCAR fined the Holman-Moody team $500 for having an oversized plate, but let the victory stand because they were unable to establish that it was used in the race.

The day before the race, typewriters clattered in the press box as writers from around the country wrote stories predicting that more than a dozen drivers were capable of winning. The restrictor plates had brought the field closer together. Baker said, "You'll be able to throw a tablecloth over the first 15 cars."

He was not far from wrong. A furious battle erupted at the front as soon as the green flag fell. It was barely 50 degrees, but most of the crowd ignored the chill as they were mesmerized by the action on the track. Nine cars broke out in a lead pack, swapping the lead almost every lap. Foyt led the first

three laps. Pearson led the fourth. Then Foyt led until Baker passed him on lap eight.

On lap nine, Maynard Troyer, a part-time racer from New York, lost control in turn two. Troyer's bright orange-red Ford hit the flat sideways at nearly full speed and began tumbling so fast, it was almost impossible to count the number of flips. Press estimates ranged from five to 18 flips. It was at least a dozen. Troyer was seriously hurt, but recovered to compete again in 1973.

After the race resumed, the lead sometimes changed two, three and even four times per lap. By lap 21, seven drivers had led. A different driver led each lap from the 20th through the 28th circuits. But trouble began to take its toll, claiming LeeRoy Yarbrough, whose oil line snapped, and Cale Yarborough, who pulled into the garage with engine problems.

The Petty Enterprises cars had started fifth and sixth. Baker immediately charged to the front, but Petty did not lead until lap 59. He was more comfortable running just out of the lead.

Just before the halfway point, the battle at the front included Foyt, Pearson, defending champion Pete Hamilton, Donnie Allison and Dick Brooks, who was driving a 1969 Dodge Daytona, the only winged car in the field. Brooks took the lead on lap 96, gave it up to Hamilton on lap 97, and took it back on lap 98. On the next lap, Brooks began to lose control in turn two. He backed off and was recovering when Hamilton tapped him. Brooks spun and collected Hamilton. Both drivers continued but were no longer a factor.

During the second half of the race, Foyt and Petty began to take control, although Donnie Allison and Baker remained in contention. Petty took the lead from Foyt on lap 103 and led 41 of the next

48 laps. But when Foyt took the lead on lap 152, he clearly had the car to beat. Foyt scorched the track, but his speed may have sealed his doom. At the end of lap 161, just after he saw the "PIT" sign from the Wood Brothers, his car began to sputter. It was out of gas. Foyt coasted around the track to the pits. The normally flawless Wood Brothers were stunned but managed to get Foyt back out only one lap down.

A few laps later, Hamilton's engine let go, prompting a yellow flag. During the caution period, Allison's car suddenly turned hard right into the tri-oval wall. His rear end had locked up. He was out of it. Foyt had passed Petty to make up his lap, but couldn't break Petty's draft. Foyt was stuck almost a full lap behind.

It was down to Baker and Petty. Baker, however, was unable to challenge. Baker had asked his crew, against their wishes, to loosen his chassis during his final stop. When the race resumed, Baker knew immediately that he had made a mistake. His car was too loose. Baker's car began sliding in the turns, and with 15 laps to go, he had to back off. For the first time in the race, one car led by more than a car length. Petty quickly opened up a big lead and won by 10 seconds. Baker and Foyt were the only other drivers to finish all 200 laps.

Petty was now a three-time winner of the Daytona 500. No other driver had won more than once. He was in his prime in a growing sport that was entering a new era. Petty went on to have one of his greatest years in 1971, winning 21 races as he captured his third NASCAR Grand National championship.

BELOW: Driving the only winged car in the field, Dick Brooks spins out on lap 98 while battling for the lead, ending his chance for victory. Brooks recovered to finish seventh, two laps down.

1972

THE YEAR 1972 MARKED THE BEGINNING OF THE MODERN ERA in NASCAR Winston Cup stock car racing. NASCAR President Bill France, 62, stepped from the limelight and turned the day-to-day operations over to his 38-year-old son, William C. France, known as "Bill Jr." His youngest son, Jim, 27, was with International Speedway Corp. But the elder France made one final master-stroke before stepping into the background.

Working with officials of the R. J. Reynolds Tobacco Co., France overhauled the Grand National series and created a leaner Winston Cup series that focused on the big races. Gone were all races under 250 miles. Thirteen short tracks were dropped, including Bowman-Gray (Winston-Salem, N.C.), Islip (N.Y.), Hickory (N.C.) and the circuits in Columbia and Greenville, S.C. The schedule was reduced from 46 to 31 races. The points system was changed. And Winston began pouring millions of dollars into the sport.

The direction was set for decades to come, but the changes had little impact on 1972 Speedweeks. Daytona was still feeling the effects of the factory withdrawals. Ford had left in 1971 and Chrysler had scaled back to the two Petty Enterprises cars. At season's end, Chrysler pulled out entirely. As a result, Junior Johnson and Banjo Matthews had stopped fielding cars. Holman-Moody, the old Ford powerhouse, struggled through an acrimonious 1971 season before the two owners ended their partnership.

When the track opened for practice, privateers dominated the garage. Thirty-one of the 69 cars in the Twin 125s were entered by independent drivers who owned their own cars. To help pick up the slack, Charlotte Motor Speedway President Richard Howard entered a pair of cars and hired Johnson to manage the team. Johnson recruited Bobby Allison, who brought $80,000 from Coca-Cola. Johnson said of sponsorship: "You've got to have it to race and we'll have it this way."

The Pettys also found help. On the heels of the Chrysler pullout, the family announced in January that it had struck a deal with STP President Andy Granatelli, which launched a sponsorship that lasted almost 30 years.

A. J. Foyt returned with the Wood Brothers team. Foyt brought sponsorship money from Purolator. At 37, Foyt was already a legend in American automobile racing. In 1967, he became a three-time winner of the Indianapolis 500, joining Wilbur Shaw, Mauri Rose and Louis Meyer. The same year, he and Dan Gurney co-drove a Ford GT to victory at Le Mans.

Foyt had been racing in NASCAR races since 1963. Although he competed in only a few races each year, Foyt loomed as a contender almost every time he showed up. After losing the 1971 Daytona 500 when he ran out of gas, Foyt won the inaugural NASCAR race at Ontario (Ca.) Motor Speedway two weeks later. In April, he won the Atlanta 500.

"He was probably the best Indy car driver of the whole bunch to come south and run the stock cars," said Junior Johnson. Richard Petty said, "He fit right in with us."

Foyt's No. 21 Mercury was the fastest in practice, but the pole went to Bobby Isaac, whose lap of 186.632 mph was his fastest of the week. Foyt was second at 184.804 mph. Speeds were again creeping up.

Isaac cruised to victory in the first Twin 125 after Petty and Buddy Baker dropped out with mechanical problems. Privateer Friday Hassler died in a 12-car accident on the backstretch. In the second race, Allison passed Foyt on the second lap and led the rest of the way, winning by 6.7 seconds. Foyt was slowed by a tire problem.

On the eve of the 500, six drivers were considered fast enough to win: Allison, Foyt, Isaac, Petty, Baker and Charlie Glotzbach. But one acted more confident than the rest. Readers of the *News-Journal* were greeted on race morning with the headline: *A. J. Foyt Says He'll Win Daytona 500 Today.*

Isaac's crew chief, Harry Hyde, believed that his driver had the edge. Isaac's Dodge Charger was built "especially for here and Talladega," Hyde said. "Aerodynamically, we have made it as slick as possible." That was a relatively new concept. But Isaac's engine began skipping on the pace lap. By lap 15, Isaac was in the pits. He dropped out after only 19 laps.

Foyt took the lead on the first lap, with Allison on his bumper. They began exchanging the lead. Baker and Petty, meanwhile, were slicing through the field. They had started 31st and 32nd because of their poor finishes in the first qualifying race. By lap three, Petty and Baker were fifth and sixth.

On lap 18, they steamrolled past Allison. But on the next lap, as they swept off turn four, Baker's car was clipped by the Ford driven by Walter Ballard, who had already been lapped once. Baker crashed into the wall and was through. Ballard's car flipped on its roof and tumbled through the tri-oval grass. It flipped three times, shedding its windshield, front bumper and other parts as it rolled. It stopped on its wheels. Ballard crawled out and trotted away unhurt.

During the caution period that followed, Allison came to the pits with valve problems. He eventually lost a cylinder and finished 23 laps down. When the race resumed, Petty and Foyt exchanged the lead nine times between laps 21 and 81.

But on lap 81, Petty slowed, drove down pit road and turned into the garage. A valve spring had broken. His race was over. After Petty's departure, Foyt was on his own. He led the rest of the way. And he won the Daytona 500 with the fastest speed and by the widest margin in the history of the race. When Foyt flashed across the finish line, averaging 161.550 mph, he was almost two laps ahead of Glotzbach.

Afterward, Foyt told the press: "You put me on the spot with that 'I'll win it' quote. I had to run harder to keep my word. It's been a dream of mine since I got into stock car racing. I've won at Indy three times and I've won at Le Mans. I've always wanted to win the Daytona 500 because I feel this is the greatest stock car race in the world."

Two weeks later, Foyt won again at Ontario. It was his seventh victory in the Winston Cup series and his last. But Foyt continued competing in NASCAR stock car races until 1994 when, at age 59, he became the oldest qualifier for the inaugural Brickyard 400 stock car race at Indianapolis Motor Speedway.

OPPOSITE: In victory lane, Foyt is interviewed by Motor Racing Network announcer Hal Hamrick. "This may have looked easy, but it wasn't," Foyt said. "I had two or three close calls out there."
BELOW: The Wood Brothers perform a pit stop on their No. 21 Ford as Foyt tosses an empty water cup out the window. Foyt's victory gave the Wood Brothers their third triumph in the Daytona 500.

1973

ON THE EVE OF THE 1973 ĐAYTONA 500, 32-year-old Buddy Baker believed it was finally his year. He had won his first 500 pole at 185.662 mph and then charged to victory in his Twin 125 after a spirited duel with Cale Yarborough. The 1973 race would be his 12th 500, and he had led in five of them.

Baker had a new ride in the K&K Insurance 1972 Dodge owned by Nord Krauskopf, one of the most successful NASCAR car owners. Bobby Isaac had won 33 races in Krauskopf's cars since 1969, as well as the 1970 NASCAR Grand National championship.

By 1972, though, Isaac was struggling. And Baker was ready to leave Petty Enterprises. Baker had run well during his two years there, with a victory each season. He had finished second to Richard in the 1971 Daytona 500. But it was a part-time ride—18 starts a year. Baker wanted more.

At Darlington before the 1972 Southern 500, in which he drove a Petty Enterprises Dodge, Baker worked out a deal to run two races for Krauskopf as Isaac's teammate. Isaac crashed on lap 12 of the race and finished last. The next day, Isaac resigned. "I don't think we need to be running two cars when we can't keep one together," he said.

Baker promptly left Petty Enterprises and took over Isaac's car. Baker finished the 1972 season with a victory in the Texas 500. And when the teams returned to Daytona for 1973 Speedweeks, Baker was just as fast as he had been in 1972.

Baker seemed to be the class of the field, but others were fast, too. Richard Petty arrived with a Fu Manchu mustache and a new 1973 Dodge. Cale Yarborough was back after a disappointing two years in Indy car racing. Yarborough took over the Richard Howard Chevy prepared by Junior Johnson. A. J. Foyt and Bobby Allison brought their own cars. David Pearson, in the Wood Brothers Ford, was a favorite on the strength of his stunning success in 1972. He had won six races in only 17 starts, including the Firecracker 400, the Winston 500 at Talladega and the Rebel 400 at Darlington.

Baker won the first Twin 125, fighting off the effects of an ear infection. A 26-year-old Tennessee driver named Darrell Waltrip had one of the most impressive runs. Driving his own 1971 Mercury, Waltrip finished sixth and captured the 11th starting spot for his first Daytona 500.

However, another Tennessee driver stole the spotlight that day. Clifton "Coo Coo" Marlin, a 41-year-old journeyman whose best finish in four previous 500s was 18th, shocked the crowd by passing David Pearson with six laps to go to win the second Twin 125. As Marlin celebrated in victory

lane with his crew and family, his 15-year-old son, Sterling, beamed with pride and dreamed of following in his father's footsteps.

Petty, who had finished fourth in the first Twin 125, wasn't happy with his Dodge until his crew made major suspension changes the day before the race. "I think we've corrected our problems," Petty said. Some Chevy owners, meanwhile, believed new NASCAR rules regarding carburetors had ruined their chances. Although Yarborough had finished second in the first qualifying race driving a Chevrolet, Johnson said, "We have about as much of a chance as a one-legged man in a sack race."

Race morning dawned gray and rainy. Baker was so ready, he didn't know if he could wait another day. The sky

remained gray, but the race got underway. Baker led the first 33 laps as Yarborough, Petty, Isaac and Pearson clung tenaciously to him. Petty led for the first time on lap 37. But as the race continued, Baker took over. He took the lead from Isaac on lap 40 and led 17 circuits. Then he led laps 71 through 102 before Yarborough squeezed past. But Baker took over again on lap 109.

By this time, Petty was out of sequence with the field. He cut a right rear tire on lap 88 and was forced to the pits. He lost a lap. He would make up the lap when the leaders pitted, but lose it again when he pitted.

With 50 laps to go, Baker was in front. He had dominated, leading 119 of the first 150 circuits, even as Yarborough stubbornly hung with him. As usual, engine problems took their toll. Pete Hamilton, who had qualified second, was first out on lap 33. Pearson's engine expired after 63 laps. Allison's and Marlin's engines also blew.

On lap 155, John Utsman's engine blew and he spun just past the finish line. Petty was back on the lead lap with Baker, but about to head for the pits. Petty just missed the spinning car. The yellow flag gave Petty another break. It allowed him to pit with Baker and remain on the lead lap. Meanwhile, Yarborough's engine quit during the caution period. He was out of the race.

RIGHT: Richard Petty battles with David Pearson in the Wood Brothers Ford early in the 1973 race. Pearson started 20th and led only one lap, the 59th circuit. Five laps later, his engine blew. He finished 33rd in the 40-car field.

BELOW: Twenty-three of the 40 cars in the 1973 race move through the tri-oval toward the line in front of packed grandstands. Media estimates placed the size of the crowd at a record 103,000.

Yarborough had led six times for 25 laps and his spirited challenge of Baker had kept the fans entertained all afternoon.

Now it was down to Baker and Petty. They were the only drivers still on the lead lap. Baker led laps 156 through 184, but both drivers needed one more quick stop for fuel. Petty came in first. He waited until the last moment before diving off turn four on lap 189 and screaming into his pit. Petty's car spewed tire smoke as he slid to a perfect stop. Five gallons and 8.4 seconds later, Petty was on his way.

Baker came in the next lap. He did not enter the pits as quickly. His stop took 9.9 seconds. When both cars reached full speed, Petty had a 4.4-second lead. Baker immediately began closing the gap, driving his car as fast as it would go. With six laps remaining, he was only 2.5 seconds behind. Suddenly, Baker's engine blew. It was over.

Petty won his fourth Daytona 500 by more than two laps. Isaac finished second, followed by Dick Brooks, three laps down. Baker's 194 circuits gave him sixth. Waltrip finished his first 500 in 12th.

Petty had been in victory circle quite a while, and had been given a big kiss by Granatelli before Baker could speak. Finally, Baker said quietly, "I can't believe it. I just can't believe it. I had it won. I haven't gotten over the shock yet. I still think I'm leading the race." Baker had come close once again, but his dance with the Daytona 500 was really just beginning.

ABOVE: Petty's pit crew gives him a fast stop under the green flag during the 1973 race. A key to his victory was a speedy fuel-only pit stop of 8.4 seconds with just 11 laps to go.

1974

OPPOSITE: Petty, who started second, leads pole winner David Pearson early in the 1974 Daytona 500 as five cars speed through turn four. Pearson led only five laps and retired after 61 circuits with a damaged exhaust system.

ABOVE: Race fans walk on the track in the tri-oval as the sun sets following another classic Daytona battle. Although the first 20 laps were sacrificed to the energy crisis, and another 53 laps were run under caution, the race still produced 60 lead changes among 15 drivers.

THE ENERGY CRISIS DOMINATED THE NEWS as 1974 Speedweeks got underway. The Oil Producing and Exporting Countries (OPEC) had cut the flow of oil to Europe and the United States, and supplies were dwindling. President Richard Nixon ordered gas stations closed from 9 p.m. Saturday to midnight Sunday each week.

Bill France swiftly responded to the crisis. He announced that the 24 Hours of Daytona was cancelled and that all Speedweeks races, including the 500, were to be cut 10 percent. In 1974, the Daytona 500 was destined to be the Daytona 450. Once again, France was ahead of the game. The sacrifice was real but small, and it reaped huge political dividends. The racing was not significantly affected and, as it turned out, the crowd was as big as ever.

David Pearson arrived at Daytona with mixed feelings. The Wood Brothers had prepared a new 1973 Mercury. But with his old '71 Mercury, Pearson had dominated the superspeedways in 1973, winning 11 races in 18 starts. Any doubts Pearson had about his new car evaporated when he won the pole with a speed of 185.017 mph, more than 3 mph faster than anyone except Richard Petty, who was second at 183.176 mph. "I hated to give up the old car," Pearson said. "But this one seems to be just about as quick and may be even stronger before the week is out."

Both Pearson and Petty were nonfactors in their Twin 125s (cut to 112.5 miles). Pearson cut a right rear tire and dropped out after 30 laps. Petty blew his engine. That opened the door for Bobby Isaac and Cale Yarborough.

Isaac was coming off a six-month 'retirement' that had begun on the 90th lap of the Talladega 500 the previous August, when he suddenly pulled into the pits, got out of his car and retired. "Something told me to quit," he said to car owner Bud Moore.

Isaac led the final 17 laps of the first Twin 125 in his Banjo Matthews Chevrolet, holding off sports-car veteran George Follmer. "I never knew how much racing meant to me until I had a chance to sit and watch it," Isaac said afterward. In the second race, Yarborough took the lead on lap 31 and was still in front with three laps to go when a yellow flag ended the contest.

Yarborough said he felt more confident on the eve of this race than ever before. The Allison brothers were also eager to go. They had finished third (Donnie) and fourth (Bobby) in the first qualifying race, and by the end of practice two days later, they were even faster. Bobby was driving his own

1974 Chevy, and Donnie was behind the wheel of the DiGard Racing 1974 Chevy. It was DiGard's first start in the 500. Donnie had failed to qualify the DiGard Chevy in 1973.

The field included Indy car drivers Tony and Gary Bettenhausen, Foyt, Johnny Rutherford, Dick Simon and Jim Hurtubise. And Darrell Waltrip was competing in his second 500, starting 11th in his own 1973 Chevy.

In response to the energy crisis the number of laps run in the race was reduced from 200 to 180. The official record shows 200 laps completed, although the race actually started on lap 21. Once the race got underway, there was no shortage of action. In fact, it had never been so competitive. Nine drivers traded the lead 21 times during the first 50 laps. Sometimes five different drivers would lead during a single lap. No one led more than seven laps in a row. Almost everyone was fast, including unlikely contenders Cecil Gordon and James Hylton. Waltrip led lap 76 to become the 10th different leader. It was the first time he had ever led the 500.

Pearson led five laps early, but was never a factor. He wheeled his new car to the garage after 61 laps with a damaged exhaust system. It was his 15th Daytona 500, and his 15th disappointment.

Petty led for the first time on lap 64. Charging to the front time and again were the Allison brothers, first Bobby, then Donnie, swapping the lead among themselves and others as gusts of winds swept the track on a blustery afternoon. But on lap 97, Bobby's engine blew.

Gradually, it became a two-car contest between Petty's Dodge and Donnie Allison's Chevy. On lap 101, they began to pull away. Between lap 120 and 180, they traded the lead 15 times, leading the field by as much as 14 seconds.

On lap 181, Petty cut his left front tire in the third turn. He was fortunate to maintain control and managed to drop off the banking and head straight to the pits. Petty didn't lose a lap, but by the time he got back up to speed, he was almost 37 seconds behind.

Allison was now in firm control. On lap 188, he became the first driver to lead 10 consecutive laps in the race. The next time around, as Allison's car screamed toward the line, smoke erupted ahead of

RIGHT: Richard Petty and Hershel McGriff lead a 32-car field to the green flag for the start of the second Twin 125 qualifying race in 1974. Petty blew his engine and fell out after 26 laps. Cale Yarborough, driving just behind Petty, led the last 20 laps and won the race.

ABOVE: A victorious Petty celebrates his fifth Daytona 500 victory in Victory Lane with his family. From left are Kyle, who holds his father's helmet, Richard, Sharon, Lynda and Lisa.

him in the tri-oval. It was Bob Burcham's engine. He was four laps down. A moment later, Allison ran over Burcham's debris. Allison's right rear tire exploded like a bomb, sending chunks of rubber high into the air. He spun into the grass by the short chute into turn one.

Allison had not hit anything, but he had to drive all the way back around the track on the rim. During the pit stop, an air wrench hose was yanked from its connection. The lug nuts on one tire had to be manually tightened. By the time Allison returned to the track, he was a lap down to Petty and out of it.

Petty breezed through the final 11 laps to win by almost a full lap—47 seconds—over Yarborough, who had fallen back after his own tire went flat. Allison finished sixth, but was stoic about the loss. "I was running so good that I was beginning to feel sorry for Richard," he said. "Then, before I knew it, I was feeling more sorry for myself."

The race had produced a record 15 leaders who swapped the lead 60 times—another record. And yet the champion once more was Petty. He had won back-to-back 500s for the first time. It was his fifth 500 victory and his third in four years.

"This is a hard race, and you have to be both good and lucky to win 'er," Petty said in victory lane. "We've been both, which is the only way I can explain why we've won five and no one else has won more than one." That said, Petty aimed his sights on number six. But the next one would not be as quick in coming.

1975

THE DISAPPOINTMENT OF 1974 DID NOT AFFECT Donnie Allison come 1975 Speedweeks. Allison won the pole position for the 1975 Daytona 500 at a speed of 185.827 mph and established himself as one of the drivers to beat. But the usual contenders were also back in force. And with the easing of the energy crisis, the race had been restored to its full 500 miles.

David Pearson, still winless in the 500, returned with the Wood Brothers and qualified second. Buddy Baker, another driver with a surplus of hard luck in the 500, was third fastest. Richard Petty was fourth fastest and ready to go for win number six.

Also in the top 10 were Bobby Allison, who had won the season opener at Riverside in his Roger Penske-owned 1975 AMC Matador, and Darrell Waltrip, who was beginning his first full season after 16 starts in 1974. Benny Parsons, the 1973 Winston Cup champion, was seventh fastest, quietly building speed in his 1975 Chevy in the shadow of the more famous drivers.

But Parsons began having problems, and when his rear end failed only seven laps into the first Twin 125, he slipped further back in the shadows. Donnie Allison lasted only nine laps before heading to the garage with an oil leak. "We've been having this problem all week," the pole winner said.

Bobby Allison won the first race by 1.6 seconds over Dick Brooks. In the second Twin 125, Pearson fashioned a slingshot pass of Petty on the last lap and won by a car length. Cale Yarborough was third.

As the 40 cars lined up on pit row for the 17th running of the 500, no two front-row starters were more determined to change their luck at Daytona than Donnie Allison and David Pearson, who said, "My luck just hasn't been too good in the 500. It's going to change."

Back in the 32nd and 33rd starting positions, Parsons and Waltrip were just hoping to avoid trouble while working their way up through the pack. Although saddled with a poor starting position, Parsons was unusually nervous before the race. He found it difficult to eat or sleep. When he finally did sleep, he had a dream that he won the race.

Parsons was 33, but he had been driving in the Winston Cup series only since 1970. He was easygoing, likable, and articulate. A native of Wilkes County, North Carolina, Parsons spent his summers with his parents in Detroit and his winters in North Carolina. He worked for a time on a Chevrolet assembly line and drove a cab for his father's small cab company. He began racing in the Automobile

OPPOSITE: A grimy but giddy Benny Parsons celebrates in victory lane with Terry Strickland, Miss Speedweeks of 1975. Parsons only led four laps during the race, including the final three circuits. The 500 was his only victory during the 1975 season.

ABOVE: Dave Marcis, driving the No. 71 K&K Insurance Dodge, leads a pack of mostly lesser-known drivers during the second Twin 125 qualifying race in 1975. Marcis is trailed by Ed Negre in the No. 0 Dodge, Walter Ballard in the No. 30 Chevy, Ferrel Harris in the No. 82 Dodge, Cale Yarborough, and Dick May in the No. 79 Dodge.

RIGHT: Six cars battle in a tight pack early in the race. Buddy Baker leads, followed by David Pearson, Cale Yarborough, Dick Brooks, Bobby Allison, and Darrell Waltrip, who was making his third start in the 500. Waltrip fell out after 54 laps with a broken axle.

Racing Club of America (ARCA) stock car series in 1963.

Daytona had been a dream even before Parsons made his first visit in 1963. Privateer driver H.B. Bailey's wife gave him a pit pass "so I got to go over and watch 'em pump gas." He made a single Winston Cup start in 1964, but didn't return to the series for five years. In 1969, he won the 300-mile ARCA race at Daytona, which helped pave the way for a full-time Winston Cup ride with car owner L.G. DeWitt in 1970.

Parsons only had two career victories, but his smooth, consistent driving had allowed him to out-last his rivals for the 1973 Winston Cup championship, which he won over Cale Yarborough. But he was winless in 1974 and nearly quit after the season ended. Parsons was not considered a threat to win the 500, particularly from his 32nd starting spot. Even worse, his engine builder, Waddell Wilson, was having nothing but trouble with the new small-block engine they were using, and did not expect it to survive 500 miles.

Pole winner Donnie Allison led the first lap, but none after that. He began having fuel flow problems and was gone by lap 36 because of a broken fuel pump. On lap three, with much of the field still tightly bunched, Jim Vandiver lost control of his car and spun in turn three. Nine cars crashed out of the race and driver J. D. McDuffie received a fractured breastbone. Parsons snaked through unscathed.

Petty had the fastest car, leading 51 of the first 74 laps. But by lap 77, Petty's car was overheating. There was a small crack in the radiator, and he was losing water. He had to pit time and again to fill the radiator. Petty was still fast on the track, but his unscheduled stops eventually put him eight laps down.

After Petty fell back, Buddy Baker dominated the middle stages of the race, leading 46 laps until a timing chain broke while he was in front. "We had this one won," Baker said. Now Pearson inherited the lead. "It was ours to win then," Pearson admitted later. "All I had to do was avoid making any mistakes." Pearson, driving the distinctive No. 21 Purolator Ford, took the lead on lap 144 and led 53 of the next 54 laps.

With 10 laps to go, Pearson had a 10-second advantage over Parsons, who had gradually moved to the front. But Parsons needed drafting help to mount any challenge to Pearson. He tried to hook up with Lennie Pond, but that didn't help. Then Petty left the pits after the last of his many stops and came up to speed near Parsons. Petty gave Parsons the "follow me" hand signal, and off they went.

Petty and Parsons gained a second a lap on Pearson, whose crew told him to pick up the pace. With less than four laps to go, the gap was down to 2.1 seconds and the fans were on their feet.

On the backstretch on lap 197, Pearson pulled low to pass the lapped cars of Cale Yarborough and Richie Panch. He had no time to waste. As he passed Yarborough and pulled in front, his right rear fender clipped Yarborough's left front. Suddenly, Pearson was sideways and spinning down the backstretch. The crowd was stunned. Parsons was as well. "The 21 car never spins!" Parsons said to himself. He was into the third turn before he realized: "I'm going to win the Daytona 500!"

The popular, warmhearted, driver received a huge welcome from members of other teams as he came down pit road. "There aren't words to describe this," Parsons said. "When I saw Richard coming up, I said, 'I hope this is the answer to my prayers.'"

In the garage, Pearson could barely tolerate questions. "I got spun out," he said, "but I'd just as soon not talk about it. People who were watching know who did it. They know who was over there with me."

One year later, it would happen to Pearson again, with a much different result.

BELOW: Nine cars crashed in turn four on the fourth lap when Jim Vandiver lost control and spun into the pack. Among those involved are Dick Trickle (75), J. D. McDuffie (70) and Grant Adcox (41). Only McDuffie was injured.

1976

ABOVE: Standing beside his wrecked car in victory lane, the grimy Pearson is interviewed. It was a different era, with fans literally hanging over the Victory Lane sign as they get a close-up view of the festivities. **BELOW:** Never had a car in this condition won in the Daytona 500. After his victory, Pearson ran in seven more Daytona 500s. His best finish was eighth in 1983.

THE SPEEDWEEKS THAT LED TO THE DAYTONA 500'S most incredible finish started in controversy. After A. J. Foyt won the pole at 187.477 mph, NASCAR inspectors began poking around the inside of his Chevy, much to the dismay of the crew. They found a bottle of nitrous oxide to give the engine a boost of horsepower. NASCAR disallowed Foyt's qualification run. NASCAR also disallowed the time of the second fastest driver, Dave Marcis, after discovering a movable flap inside the grille that channeled air away from the nose of the car to improve aerodynamics. And they disqualified the third fastest driver, Darrell Waltrip, after discovering a nitrous bottle inside his car.

The cars of Foyt, Marcis and Waltrip had qualified considerably faster than anyone else. Waltrip frankly admitted, "If you don't cheat, you look like an idiot. If you do it and don't get caught, you look like a hero. If you do it and get caught, you look like a dope. Put me in the category where I belong."

After the disqualifications, Ramo Stott took the pole by default with a speed of 183.456 mph. But Marcis and Waltrip gained a measure of redemption when they won the Twin 125s.

Lurking just offstage during Speedweeks were a bearded Richard Petty, the five-time 500 champion, and David Pearson, whose 500s were mostly disappointments. Pearson finished third in the first Twin 125. Petty finished a distant second to Waltrip in the second race.

Nothing during Speedweeks foretold of a classic Pearson-Petty Daytona 500 duel, but their ongoing battle for supremacy stretched back into the 1960s. Pearson was two-and-a-half years older than Petty, and his apprenticeship in NASCAR racing had lasted much longer and had been far rockier. A native of Spartanburg, S.C., Pearson raced for the first time in 1952 in an outlaw hobby race in nearby Woodruff. He was 17. He won $13 and was hooked.

But Pearson couldn't get a Grand National ride in the 1950s. He spent his own money to put together a 1959 Chevrolet for the 1960 Daytona 500 and qualified 33rd. It was his first Grand National start. In 1961, Ray Fox gave Pearson a ride and Pearson won three superspeedway races. He was finally on his way.

By the late 1960s, Pearson and Petty dominated the sport. Pearson won the 1966, 1968 and 1969 Grand National championships. Petty won a record 27 races and the championship in 1967. In 1972, Pearson stopped running a full NASCAR schedule when he joined the Wood Brothers, who focused on the big races and never ran a full season until 1985. From 1972 through 1975, Pearson and the Wood Brothers became the kings of the superspeedways, winning 27 of 72 races.

But the Daytona 500 was Pearson's Achilles heel. He led for the first time in 1967, but his engine blew. He had four top-10s in the 1960s. He dominated the 1970 race, leading 82 laps, only to fall to Pete Hamilton at the end. He finished fourth in 1971. He won the pole in 1974. In 1975, Pearson led 74 laps and was in front with less than four laps to go when he tangled with the lapped car driven by Cale Yarborough and spun down the backstretch. By 1976, Pearson had raced in 16 Daytona 500s. He had a second, a third, two fourths, a fifth, and two sixths, but no trophy. Before the race he joked, "If I don't spin out, I could win."

There was tension between Pearson and Petty at Daytona. Pearson had juked Petty into a premature pass in the 1974 Firecracker 400, then repassed him to win. In the 1975 classic, Benny Parsons was no threat to Pearson until Petty assisted with his draft.

The 1976 race had an assortment of early leaders, including Terry Ryan, Jimmy Means, Terry Bivins, Jackie Rogers, and David Hobbs. A. J. Foyt and Bobby Allison were contenders until sidelined by engine failure. But in the final 100 miles, it was all Petty and Pearson. Everyone else was at least a lap down.

ABOVE: The greatest drivers of their time gather before the third running of the International Race of Champions event at Daytona. From left are David Pearson, Bobby Unser, Mario Andretti, Emerson Fittipaldi, A. J. Foyt, Benny Parsons, Al Unser, and Bobby Allison. Parsons won the race.

RIGHT: In this sequence Petty
has lost his battle to maintain
control and hits the outside
wall. Pearson spins out of
control toward pit road,
wondering all the while, "Who's
going to win this race?" Then,
as Petty begins his spin toward
the infield, Pearson is about to
hit Joe Frasson, sending
Frasson's car into a spin. Petty's
car then comes to a halt in the
infield with a stalled engine,
and it won't turn over. Pearson
limps toward the line. Petty's
crew pour over the wall in a
mad dash to help their driver.
Finally, Pearson takes the
checkered flag to win the race
as the first crewman arrives at
the back of Petty's car. The
crew's action would incur a
meaningless one-lap penalty.
Petty still finished second.

The final duel was set up by a yellow flag on lap 171. Pearson had the lead on the restart, but on lap 188, Petty swept by Pearson through the tri-oval and took over. Pearson was content to let him stay there. On the track, they appeared to be evenly matched. But both drivers sensed that Petty had a slight edge.

Recalls Leonard Wood, "David radioed in and said he was wide open. He said that was all he could do, which was typical of him. He'd rather say he couldn't rather than he could. But we still felt like he was going to try to pass him."

Pearson decided that his only chance to make a pass stick was to wait until the final lap. Down the backstretch they went for the final time, as a record crowd of 125,000 stood and roared. Pearson made his pass on the straightaway. He was leading as they entered the third turn. Pearson was in the high groove. Petty moved low after they passed a lapped car. As they sped through the fourth turn, Petty executed a slow-motion pass below Pearson. Petty was nearly past Pearson as they came off the corner. His car drifted up and his right rear fender touched Pearson's left front fender.

Pearson jerked the wheel left, then right, to try to maintain control, but his car went hard right and straight into the wall. He had the presence of mind to push the clutch in to keep from stalling. Petty's car fishtailed right, left, right and then also slammed head first into the outside wall, ahead of Pearson.

Great clouds of white tire smoke billowed as Petty's car spun into the tri-oval banking and toward the finish line. Petty thought to himself, "I'm going to be the first to win the Daytona 500 backward." But his car slid to a stop in the grass 20 yards from the line. The engine was dead. And it wouldn't crank. The radiator was pushed back into the fan.

LEFT: From a perch in the infield, male and female fans alike cheer the action. The 1976 race not only had a classic finish, but also featured 35 lead changes among 11 drivers.

Pearson's car came off the wall, spun around and slid toward the entrance to pit road. It clipped Joe Frasson's car, sending Frasson's car into a spin. Frasson's car, contrary to legend, did not knock Pearson's car back on course. Pearson screamed to his crew on the radio, "Where's Richard?"

Pearson kept the engine running, straightened his car out, and rumbled through the infield grass toward the finish line at about 30 miles per hour. Meanwhile, some of Petty's young crewmen had spilled over pit wall and were sprinting across the grass toward his car. As Pearson reached the apron, Benny Parsons motored past. "Right before David crossed the finish line, Benny blows by right ahead of us," Leonard Wood recalls. "And I think, 'Oh, my goodness, Benny's done it again.' Then we came to find out he was a lap down."

Petty, meanwhile, tried in vain to start his car. As his crewmen pushed, he threw the car into fourth gear and limped across on the starter motor. The push earned him a meaningless one-lap penalty.

There was pandemonium as Pearson drove his wrecked car down pit lane. Petty, walking back to the garage, shouted an apology to Pearson for running into him. As Pearson steered his battle-damaged Mercury into victory lane, he had his 89th career victory, and the sweetest of them all. "I've been waitin' a long time for this one," he said in the press box. "I knew when it got down to the end, ol' Richard would be there."

OPPOSITE: Pit stops during a yellow flag create a traffic jam on pit road early in the race. As mechanics work under the hood of Dave Marcis' car, Jim Vandiver parks sideways in the pit behind. Further back, Buddy Arrington and Coo Coo Marlin leave pit road, while Bruce Hill pulls in. In the distance, Richard Petty's car is serviced.
LEFT: Cale Yarborough speeds through the lengthening shadows of a February afternoon to take the checkered flag for his second Daytona 500 victory. Benny Parsons finished second, 1.39 seconds behind.
BELOW: At speed at Daytona in his Chevrolet Laguna S-3, Cale Yarborough was starting his fifth season with car owner Junior Johnson. Yarborough's victory in the 500 gave Johnson his second 500 win as a car owner.

1977

THE FIRST DRIVER TO GRAB THE SPOTLIGHT DURING 1977 SPEEDWEEKS was Donnie Allison, who had not even been in the field the year before. Allison had won the pole for the 1975 Daytona 500 as the first driver for the new DiGard Racing team, but during the summer owners Bill and Jim Gardner had let Allison go and hired Darrell Waltrip.

Allison came to Daytona in 1976 without a ride, and didn't get one. Later in the season, however, he began driving Hoss Ellington's Chevrolet, and took it to victory lane at Charlotte in October 1976. The team survived cheating allegations after that race, with Ellington telling inspectors: "This one's legal. We left all the cheater stuff at Darlington."

Now, at Daytona, Allison felt a sense of reaffirmation after winning his second pole at 188.048 mph. "What satisfies me is the knowledge that I can drive a race car as good as anybody out here," Allison said. He fended off quips about cheating by saying, "I didn't turn nothin' on or nothin' off in the car—except the ignition switch."

One of the first to congratulate Allison was Cale Yarborough, who dropped by as Allison's car went through inspection. Five days later, the spotlight shifted to Yarborough and Petty when they ran away with the Twin 125s. Allison led the first four laps of the first race, but his car was loose. He finished fifth. Petty took command on lap eight and pulled away. He finished 28.5 seconds ahead of Pearson. Bobby Allison was third. Janet Guthrie, who became the first woman to pass the rookie test at Indianapolis in 1976, finished 18th. That was good for the 39th starting spot. Guthrie was the first woman to qualify for the Daytona 500. Later that year, she became the first woman to qualify for the Indianapolis 500.

A. J. Foyt had qualified second, which put him on the pole for the second race. He led the first two laps, but Yarborough blew past Foyt on lap three and led the rest of the way, except for the one lap when he pitted. Yarborough was two seconds ahead of Benny Parsons when a yellow flag

RIGHT: Yarborough celebrates in Victory Lane with a race queen (right) and his wife, Betty Jo. Yarborough went on to win eight more races in 1997, as well as the Winston Cup championship.

flew with three laps left and the race ended under caution.

Race morning dawned cold and gloomy, but the skies cleared, bringing swirling winds that sucked trash out of the garbage cans and littered the track. As the field began the parade lap, maintenance crews were still picking up litter off the racing surface. Among the estimated 135,000 fans—another record—was Billy Carter, brother of President Jimmy Carter.

On the pace lap, Petty peeled off the track and headed to the pits with smoke from an oil leak trailing from his Dodge. He got back onto the track as the green flag fell, but started almost a lap down. At the front, there was no shortage of action. Allison led the first lap. Foyt led lap two. Pearson took over on lap three. Yarborough led lap four.

Suddenly, a fire erupted from under the dashboard of Bobby Wawak's Chevy. The flames were all over Wawak as he frantically tried to steer his car off the track. "It was like sitting in front of a blow torch," he said later. Wawak managed to unbuckle his belts and tumble from the blazing car before it stopped. He got up and sprinted to the infield hospital for help. He was seriously burned, particularly on his gloveless hands, and faced a long but successful recovery.

Yarborough led 65 of the first 100 laps, but others were strong, too, including Allison, Foyt and Baker. Waltrip led a few circuits. Petty, meanwhile, clawed his way back to the front and even led laps 61 through 64. But Petty's day ended on lap 111 when his engine blew. Donnie Allison was already gone by then, sidelined by a crash on lap 88 when he ran over parts of a blown engine and blew a tire. And Foyt soon fell back.

Trash was getting into radiators, causing engines to overheat. And the wind was still blowing briskly. Ramo Stott said he crashed on lap 108 when the wind blew him into the wall. On lap 122, Baker was in front as the lead pack steamed past the lapped car of Salt Walther on the backstretch. Suddenly Walther's car veered right and slammed into Baker's car, sending it into a spin. Yarborough, trailing Baker, turned left onto the backstretch grass to avoid a collision. He managed to maintain control as Pearson took the lead.

Baker was out of contention, but he quickly rejoined the race and eventually finished third, only one lap down. Baker was pleased with his finish, but said afterward that the accident "makes me so mad, I could just spit!" During the caution period for Baker's incident, Benny Parsons took the lead for the first time.

And when Pearson dropped out with a blown engine on lap 135, Parsons was the only driver left to challenge Yarborough. Parsons had struggled early in the race. His windshield had been hit by a rock. But the yellow flags flew at the right times for Parsons, and with 75 miles to go, he was actually in the lead. As Parsons said afterward, "All of a sudden, it was a new dream—a whole new world."

It didn't take long for reality to set in. On lap 172, Yarborough eased past Parsons and retook the lead. But Parsons hung on to Yarborough's draft and the two raced together as the laps wound down. Lap after lap, Parsons stayed on Yarborough's bumper, hoping to catch a break, or take advantage of a mistake.

Finally, with about five laps to go, Yarborough began to leave Parsons behind. Coming off turn two, a gust of wind nearly blew Parsons into the backstretch wall and he had to let off the gas. Yarborough said he broke the draft with Parsons by putting some moves on him while they were among lapped cars. Either way, Yarborough was free of his last threat and cruised under the checkered flag 1.39 seconds ahead of Parsons. Behind them, Baker finished third, a lap down. Coo Coo Marlin was fourth, two laps back, followed by Dick Brooks and Foyt. And Guthrie was still running at the end as well. She finished 12th, 12 laps behind.

With his victory, Yarborough become only the second driver to win more than one Daytona 500. And it had been quite a while since his first in 1968. He said, "I can't believe it's been nine years since I won the Daytona 500 before, because I've run every race just as hard as I did this one." He added, "A win makes up for a lot of losses."

BELOW: The Junior Johnson pit crew gives Yarborough a fast stop during the race. Johnson himself mans the jack, hopping over an air hose as he and his team prepare to change left side tires during a four-tire stop. "I won," Yarborough said afterwards, "because I had the best car on the racetrack."

1978

AS THE TRACK OPENED FOR PRACTICE TO BEGIN 1978 SPEEDWEEKS, a variety of different cars, some with less-than-pleasant handling, kept the drivers on their toes. Cale Yarborough, the defending 500 champion and two-time defending Winston Cup champion, won the pole position in an Oldsmobile 442 at 187.536 mph, but emerged from his car thoroughly spooked.

"You just would not believe how unstable the car was," Yarborough said. He ran only one practice lap before the qualifying run, explaining afterward, "Man, I couldn't hold my breath any longer than for one." Yarborough said his problem was caused by a big, open side window on his car. Richard Petty, who was driving a new Dodge Magnum, said none of the drivers knew what to expect. "That's especially true when it comes to running in traffic, when the wind currents come into play so much," he said.

The Twin 125s were delayed a day by rain. When they finally got underway, Yarborough and the other Olds and Buick drivers were relieved to discover that their cars handled better in traffic. A.J. Foyt won the first Twin 125 in a Buick, passing David Pearson with 19 laps to go. Among the drivers in the lead pack was 22-year-old Bill Elliott, a racer from the Georgia hills, who said after finishing fifth that it "was a thrill to run up front with those guys." In the second race, Darrell Waltrip led down the backstretch of the final lap, lost the lead to Petty in turn three, but repassed him in turn four to win by a car length.

Bobby Allison led four laps in the first race and was battling Buddy Baker for the lead on lap 27 when Baker lost control in turns three and four and took both cars out. Allison was driving the Bud Moore Ford Thunderbird for the first time, taking over after Baker's departure. Baker had driven Moore's car for three and a half seasons, but departed after a winless 1977. Allison, too, was looking for a fresh start after winless seasons in 1976 and 1977.

Allison was a veteran of 14 Daytona 500s. Like Baker, he had known mostly frustration. His best finish had been in 1975, when he was a distant second, one lap behind winner Benny Parsons. Allison's crash in the qualifying race relegated him to the 33rd starting position—his worst start since 1969. Baker started 31st.

Race day was cool and overcast. Yarborough, Waltrip and Petty immediately began battling for the lead after the green flag fell. Petty took the lead on lap 29 and led the next 32 circuits, carrying

Waltrip and Pearson in a three-car draft that moved away from the rest of the field.

Suddenly, on lap 61, Petty blew a tire, collecting Waltrip and Pearson. All three leaders hit the outside wall in turn four, then spun across the track toward the inside fence. They were out of it. The race had barely resumed when Benny Parsons blew a tire on the frontstretch. Foyt hit his brakes to avoid Parsons and was hit from behind by Lennie Pond. Foyt's car slid off the track and began tumbling through the grass, shedding parts and gouging chunks of sod high into the air. The car finally landed on its wheels. Foyt was briefly knocked out, but not seriously hurt.

The crashes allowed Allison and Baker to move to the front. And on lap 72, Allison took the lead for the first time. Two laps later, Baker took over. As the race wore on, Baker emerged as the strongest contender. He led all but three circuits between laps 118 and 167, building a lead of more than 42 seconds at one point.

But with less than 30 laps to go, Baker's car started vibrating. He sensed a tire going down and rushed to the pits for a change of tires as Allison went back in the lead. Even after the unscheduled stop, Baker managed to retake the lead, passing Allison on lap 187. But Allison retook the lead on lap 190. Baker's vibration continued. Now he knew it wasn't a tire.

Afterward, Baker said, "I thought a tire had gone down. But when I went back out, I knew that wasn't it. The oil pressure needle started dropping and so did my heart. It was the engine getting ready to go." On lap 195, Baker slowed as smoke began pouring from his engine.

Allison was home free, and won by 33.2 seconds over Cale Yarborough, who had been slowed by minor engine problems. One of Daytona's hard-luck drivers had finally broken through. The speedway had rewarded his years of struggle with a healthy serving of good fortune.

"We had our share of luck to get here today," Allison said. "I almost got into that mess when Benny spun and A. J. flipped on the frontstretch. Then, an orange car (driven by Ron Hutcherson) put me in the wall on the backstretch and bent the sheet metal in on the tires. I could smell the rubber burning and I figured we'd had it." But Moore and his crew had managed to pull the fenders off the tires before disaster struck.

Baker, meanwhile, confronted another bitter loss. For the fourth time, he had dominated the Daytona 500, driving to the edge of victory. For the fourth time, he came up short. Baker congratulated Allison as he rolled down pit road. Then he faced his own emotions. "Damn," he said, "what has a fellow got to do?"

OPPOSITE: With his wife, Judy, Bobby Allison hoisted the Daytona 500 winner's trophy for the first time. It had taken him 15 years, although he was the runner-up in 1975 and had two third-place finishes to show for those years.

BELOW: The pit crew of team owner Bud Moore performs a pit stop on Bobby Allison's No. 15 Ford on his way to victory in 1978. The car had a rear spoiler, a relatively new addition that is minuscule by today's standards.

1979

OPPOSITE: With Darrell Waltrip hugging his bumper, Petty takes the checkered flag to win the 1979 race. A. J. Foyt follows in third. The last lap was the only one Petty led during the second half of the race.
ABOVE: Petty in 1979, his 22nd season in the NASCAR Winston Cup series.
BELOW: Petty's sixth Daytona 500 victory was emotional because it was so unexpected. He was in the shadows during most of this race, and had only led twice for 11 laps before the dramatic final circuit.

THE 1979 DAYTONA 500 WAS THE FIRST TO BE TELEVISED LIVE from start to finish to a national television audience. It was a watershed race for another reason, too. It was Dale Earnhardt's first start. And it was the first start for two other rookies—Geoff Bodine and Terry Labonte—who would soon become household names in the Winston Cup series.

Speeds were way up in 1979. Buddy Baker set a new track record of 194.015 mph to win the pole position. Stealing the spotlight that day, however, was 18-year-old Kyle Petty, Richard's son, who had thrown a block to cover the low groove on the last lap and held off John Rezek to win the ARCA 200, the support race run on pole day. It was the first race Kyle had ever entered. Three generations of Pettys—all winners at Daytona—celebrated in victory lane.

Buddy Baker swept to victory in the first Twin 125, passing Cale Yarborough with three laps to go after making up a 4.1-second deficit in only seven laps. In the second race, Darrell Waltrip led the final 28 laps. On the final circuit, Waltrip held off A. J. Foyt, Dick Brooks and Earnhardt, who made a stab at Foyt and Waltrip, but fell to fourth. Earnhardt had already impressed the Daytona fans with his steady seventh-place finish in his first Daytona race, the 1978 Firecracker 400. His run in the Twin 125 made him a driver to watch.

Baker was the clear favorite as race day dawned warm, humid, overcast and wet. The Daytona Beach weather was still better than much of the rest of the country. Homebound by snow, millions settled in and turned on the race on CBS. Rain delayed the start and forced the first 15 laps to be run under yellow to help dry the track. Those were the only laps Baker led. His engine went sour almost as soon as the race started, and he retired after 38 laps.

The Allison brothers and Cale Yarborough were battling at the front on lap 31 when Bobby's car drifted up into Donnie's as they came off turn two. All three drivers went spinning down the backstretch grass, plowing through puddles and ponds. Although none of the cars was badly dam-

ABOVE: From the air looking east on race day, the Daytona International Speedway is jammed with the cars of thousands of race fans. Just beyond the speedway is the Daytona Beach Municipal Airport.

aged, Bobby and Cale lost three laps getting back on track, while Donnie went one lap down.

The mishap brought other drivers to the front, and on lap 44, as the leaders entered the third turn, Earnhardt stuck the nose of his blue-and-yellow Buick ahead of Neil Bonnett to lead the Daytona 500 for the first time. At that very instant, CBS announcer Ken Squier said, "Earnhardt! Now there's the kid to watch!" Earnhardt led five times for 10 laps before he lost the draft and finished eighth. Bodine and Labonte also ran well, with Bodine leading six laps.

The race was punctuated by trouble. A six-car crash in turn four on lap 54 took out David Pearson. Neil Bonnett and Harry Gant crashed on lap 74, which allowed Donnie Allison to regain his lost lap. Yarborough also was slowly gaining back his lost ground.

Parsons had a strong car and led laps 86 through 106, giving CBS viewers some of the first in-car images from a large, fixed camera mounted in his car. But Donnie Allison was soon back in the fray, and began to dominate the second half of the race. Allison led all but four of the laps between 108 and 171.

With help from yellow flags, Yarborough made up his lost laps and was ready to battle for the lead as the race entered its final 100 miles. Yarborough went into first on lap 174 as he battled with Foyt and Donnie Allison. But after the final pit stops, which came under the green flag, Allison and Yarborough hooked up in a two-car draft and began to pull away. Petty had spun his tires in the pits, which caused him to lose the lead draft. He hooked up with Foyt and Waltrip, but with just five laps left, they were a half lap behind.

Yarborough knew his car was stronger than Allison's, and was content to wait. Allison led 22 laps before the final circuit. Allison decided that if Yarborough was going to pass him, he was going to have to go high.

Yarborough had planned to make his move in turn four. But as he came off turn two, he saw Bobby Allison's lapped car way ahead, but slowing. Yarborough figured Bobby was waiting for them to catch up so he could block for his brother. Yarborough told car owner Junior Johnson on the radio: "I'm going to have a problem up here, so I'm makin' my move now." He pulled low on the backstretch.

In the television booth, Squier's voice reached a fever pitch. "It's all come down to this! Out of turn two, Donnie Allison in first. Where will Cale make his move? He comes to the inside. Donnie Allison throws the block! Cale hits him! He slides! Donnie Allison slides! They hit again! They drive into the turn! They're hitting the wall! They slide down to the inside! They are out of it!"

A half lap behind, Foyt was leading Petty and Waltrip. Foyt saw the yellow light come on and checked up. Petty and Waltrip went past. Petty wasn't sure what was up until he reached the third turn and saw Allison's car in the grass. He figured Yarborough was somewhere nearby. Through the final turn and to the flag, Petty thought of how his son had covered the low groove in the ARCA race. He put the same move on Waltrip, who touched the apron trying to get by.

On the backstretch, Yarborough and Donnie Allison began having a lively discussion. Bobby pulled up. They exchanged words. Yarborough whapped Bobby with his helmet through the window. Donnie grabbed Cale as Bobby got out of his car. Cale took a swing at Donnie and kicked at Bobby, who grabbed Yarborough's leg and wrestled him to the ground. At that point, track workers broke up the fight—the most famous in stock car racing history.

Petty's sixth Daytona 500 victory came just two months after major stomach surgery. He had led just 12 laps. He did not have the strongest car. But the victory was one of his biggest, and ended the longest winless streak of his career to that point, a 45-race drought that lasted more than a year.

The three combatants received modest fines. The race garnered huge television ratings. Ironically, in the next race at Rockingham two weeks later, Yarborough and Donnie Allison were battling for the lead on the ninth lap when they collided and spun. There was no fight this time. Both drivers said it was just a racing accident.

LEFT: After crashing together during the final lap of the 500, Cale Yarborough and Donnie Allison didn't get physical until Bobby Allison showed up. In the first image, Bobby Allison lunges at Cale's leg as rescue workers move in. Then a worker tries to restrain Cale as Donnie appears in the picture. Finally, Cale and Donnie continue to jaw at each other after the fight was broken up.

1980

BUDDY BAKER'S QUEST TO WIN THE DAYTONA 500 had begun way back in 1961, when he was just 21 years old. It took him six tries before he ever led a lap. He failed to finish in the top 10 until 1969, his eighth race. He sat on the pole for the first time that year.

The 1970s brought one heartbreak after another. He suffered a bitter loss to teammate Richard Petty in 1971 when he was outsmarted in the pits. He won the pole and led 157 laps in 1973, but his engine blew six laps from the finish. He had a half-lap lead in 1975 when his car suddenly quit. In 1978, he was leading with five laps to go when his engine went sour. In 1979, he had won the pole and dominated Speedweeks, only to have his engine start missing on the first green flag lap.

No one had a record of futility quite like Baker's, and no driver was more vocal in his desire to win the 500, or more expressive in his agony after every crushing defeat.

Yet, in 1980, Baker was more confident than ever, especially after winning the pole at 194.009 mph. But he didn't strut his stuff as he had in 1979. He laid back, just out of the spotlight. The Twin 125s were won by Donnie Allison and Neil Bonnett, although the day was marred by the death of 28-year-old Ricky Knotts in a crash in the second Twin 125. Baker finished third in the first race.

On the eve of the 500, Baker couldn't help himself. He predicted victory. Again. "I'm flying," he said. "I'm turning laps at just over 197 and I'm going to win if nothing goes wrong for a change down here." Baker was driving a silver-and-black Oldsmobile the team called "The Grey Ghost." It was owned by Harry Ranier and prepared by crew chief Waddell Wilson.

The race started under cool but sunny skies, and Baker lost no time establishing his dominance. He led 30 of the first 33 laps, then gave way for a time as Bonnett, Cale Yarborough, and Richard Petty traded the lead. Dale Earnhardt had started 32nd after blowing an engine in his Twin 125, but by lap 60, he was in front. And as the race surged into its second half, Earnhardt seemed to be the only driver capable of challenging Baker.

OPPOSITE: It seemed as if everyone wanted to share in Buddy Baker's joy as a mob of crewmen, friends, and fans piled onto his car for the ride to Victory Lane. It had taken him 18 tries to win the race.
ABOVE: Dale Earnhardt, driving the No. 2 Oldsmobile owned by Rod Osterlund, was the only driver capable of giving much of a challenge to Baker in 1980. Here, they battle side by side in turn four. Earnhardt led seven times, but only for a total of 10 laps.
LEFT: Janet Guthrie, the first woman to drive in the Daytona 500 and the Indianapolis 500, made her second and final start in the Daytona classic in 1980. She finished 11th, seven laps down, driving the Rod Osterlund Chevrolet. She had finished 12th in 1977.

From lap 88 to lap 180, Baker led all but 12 circuits. But as the race reached its final dramatic laps, he was leading a tight four-car draft with Allison, Bonnett and Earnhardt. On lap 180, Baker peeled off the track and dashed to his pit for fuel. This time, unlike 1971, Baker would not be caught flat-footed in the pits. Wilson called for a single, 11-gallon can of gas and Baker was gone in six seconds.

The others had pitted, too, but Bonnett's gas-only stop had taken 11 seconds. Allison went for two tires and took even longer. Earnhardt's tire changer failed to get the lug nuts on the left rear and he had to make another stop, losing a lap.

Baker emerged with a six-second lead over Bonnett, which he expanded to 13 seconds. But Wilson worried whether the car had enough gas. He told Baker to take it easy. "Hey, I'm not stopping, I can tell you that," Baker told Wilson. The conversation became so animated, Baker later said it sounded like "the kitchen on a busy, hectic Saturday night" at the Chinese restaurant of his fishing buddy, Junior Wong.

But there was no need to worry. This time, it all held together. The last three laps were run under caution after a blown engine oiled the track, but Baker still finished the 500 miles at a record average speed of 177.602 mph.

As he rolled toward victory lane, Baker's old crews—the Pettys, Bud Moore's boys, the M.C. Anderson team—flooded pit road to offer their congratulations. "Buddy was just tremendous," said rival Bobby Allison, who finished second. Bonnett and Earnhardt were third and fourth.

"That car was so dominant," Baker recalls. "I tell people this and they don't believe it, but I could actually back off. And that's still the fastest 500 ever run. The thing about Daytona, it's really a measure of your career. To me, the world was lifted off my shoulders after I won. Because no matter what, I had won the Daytona 500. And that registers more than names or records or anything else. Because it's something you're remembered for."

BELOW: From the photographer's stand, a wide-angle lens takes in the view as Baker is interviewed by Brock Yates for the CBS telecast. Baker ran in 18 more races in 1980 and also won the Winston 500 at Talladega.

1981

IN THE WAKE OF THE ENERGY CRISES OF THE 1970S, Americans demanded smaller cars and Detroit began building them. NASCAR joined the trend in 1981 and ordered down-sized cars for the Winston Cup series by shortening the wheelbase from 115 to 110 inches. Most of the models were boxy, with severely sloped rear windows. At 190 mph, they were a handful. The air current over the cars created vacuums over the trunks that lightened the rear ends and made them wickedly loose. Darrell Waltrip said it was like driving on a crowded freeway at 70 mph with flat tires. "It scares me tee-totally, absolutely to death," he said. One mechanic said he saw daylight under Cale Yarborough's tires as the Oldsmobile came off turn four.

During winter testing, most teams reached the same conclusion—their new cars were fast but handled poorly. Bobby Allison, who replaced Buddy Baker at Ranier Racing, tested an Oldsmobile and was not happy with the results. Allison's crew chief, Waddell Wilson, noticed that the Pontiac LeMans was on NASCAR's list of approved cars and that its back roof was far less sloped than the other cars.

Secretly, the Ranier team went to work. A dozen men worked over the winter, sometimes seven days a week, to get the new car finished. They named their car "Silver Streak," and Allison took it out on the first day of practice and posted the fastest lap. Then he won the pole at 194.624 mph. Allison had no complaints about his handling.

Other teams cried foul. NASCAR Technical Director Bill Gazaway was unsympathetic. The other teams were "outfoxed," he said, "And you're going to have a heck of a time getting any of them to admit it." At the same time, he ordered a rule change allowing the teams to run with larger rear spoilers to increase stability. And after the Twin 125s, NASCAR increased the size again. In five days, the spoiler went from 216 to 250 to 276 square inches.

The second rule change was prompted by the wild action in the first Twin 125. As Allison drove to victory, leading 33 laps, the race was slowed by two scary crashes. John Anderson spun off turn two on lap 28. His car lifted off the ground, did a reverse half

ABOVE: Dale Earnhardt leads Richard Petty through the tri-oval during the 1981 race. Earnhardt led twice for four laps and finished fifth, the last car on the lead lap.

BELOW: With crew chief Dale Inman changing the right front tire, the pit crew of Richard Petty services his 1981 Buick during the 500. Inman's decision to not change any tires on the final stop paved the way for Petty's seventh victory.

roll, landed on its roof and began tumbling violently forward. It flipped six times, but Anderson was not seriously injured. The race ended under caution after Connie Saylor spun off the same turn, lifted off and slid down the backstretch on his roof.

In the second race, Waltrip drove to the apron off turn four and bullied his way past Benny Parsons to win. Parsons said if he hadn't lifted, Waltrip "was going to crash 12 cars." Waltrip was roundly criticized by the other drivers, including Petty, who said, "Darrell done one of the stupidest things today I've ever seen anybody do in racing in almost a quarter-century career."

Dark clouds gathered over the speedway on race weekend, drowning Saturday's Sportsman 300. The mood before the 500 was as dark as the weather. Waltrip spoke of "hanging onto the steering wheel for dear life as much as for driving." Said Baker, "It's like driving into the unknown."

Perhaps the drivers were scared into driving safely, or maybe it was simply racing fate. But the 1981 Daytona 500 was trouble-free except for four yellow flags for minor incidents. The day was cool, overcast and windy, but the race was fast, clean and extremely competitive, with 49 lead changes among nine drivers during the first 175 laps. There was much passing, but very little side-by-side driving. And it was Allison who was up front most often. Time and time again—20 times in all— Allison stuck the nose of his LeMans in front. He led a total of 90 laps. Neil Bonnett was one of Allison's fiercest competitors, leading 15 different times for 26 laps. But Bonnett was doomed by tire trouble, as was Cale Yarborough. Waltrip, A. J. Foyt and David Pearson blew their engines.

As the final round of pit stops loomed under the green flag, Allison took the lead from Baker on lap 167 and moved ahead by about 10 car lengths. Seven laps later, Allison slowed on the backstretch. Baker and Dale Earnhardt sped past. Allison was out of gas. Allison had to coast almost half a lap to

OPPOSITE: In Victory Lane, a triumphant Richard Petty lifts his grandson, Adam, as Lynda Petty looks on with admiration. Adam was less than a year old, having been born July 10, 1980, to Kyle and Pattie Petty.
BELOW: As the laps wind down in the race, crew chief Dale Inman carefully watches the lap times as a CBS cameraman moves in to cover the finish. Afterward, during a television interview, Inman emotionally spoke of the family sacrifices it took to win.

the pits. It cost him the race. Baker and Earnhardt also ran out of gas as they hit pit road. All three drivers changed right-side tires. Allison's stop took 17.4 seconds. Baker was out in 15.3 seconds; Earnhardt in 15.2 seconds.

On lap 176, Petty hurtled into the pits. "They're not changing tires!" CBS pit reporter Ned Jarrett shouted into his microphone. "A change of pace there for the Petty crew. They're only adding gasoline and he's away! A very quick stop. What strategy! We'll see how it works."

Petty's 6.8-second stop worked just fine. He emerged with a lead of about six seconds over Baker, Ricky Rudd and Earnhardt. Allison trailed by another two seconds. Allison closed the gap and clawed his way to second, but at the checkered flag, Petty was 3.5 seconds ahead. Rudd finished third, followed by Baker and Earnhardt.

It was victory number seven for Petty—a joyous ending to a difficult week. Not only had the car been a handful, it had lunched two engines, and engine builder Maurice Petty had been forced to return to the Petty shop in Level Cross, N.C., to do additional engine work. Afterward, as the family celebrated in victory lane, his wife, Lynda, held grandson Adam, who mugged for the camera and tried to grab an announcer's microphone.

"We've won 500s where we outran 'em, where we out-lucked 'em, where we've out-everythinged 'em," Petty said. "Now you can add a new one. We out-thunk 'em."

1982

BOBBY ALLISON'S DISAPPOINTMENT AFTER HIS LOSS in the 1981 Daytona 500 did not soon abate. Within a month, new NASCAR rules for the spoiler of his fast Pontiac LeMans had rendered the car obsolete. Allison and car owner Harry Ranier switched to a Buick. Allison won five races, but left the team at the end of the season and took over the DiGard Buick.

DiGard Racing had flourished with Darrell Waltrip from 1975 through 1980, but a winless 1981 season with Ricky Rudd prompted the switch to Allison. Meanwhile, Benny Parsons took over for Allison at Ranier Racing and convinced crew chief Waddell Wilson to switch back to the LeMans that had so dominated the 1981 race. Parsons made good on his recommendation by stealing the pole for the 1982 race at a record speed of 196.317 mph. It was the fourth straight 500 pole for Ranier Racing, spread among three drivers. Parsons' run had eclipsed the old mark of 196.049 mph set by Buddy Baker in winning Ranier's first pole in 1979.

But Allison put on his own show after qualifications. He started 12th in a field of 13 cars in the Busch Clash, a 20-lap sprint inaugurated in 1979 as the first race of Speedweeks. Allison passed five cars on the first lap, took the lead on lap five and held off a last-lap challenge from Neil Bonnett, who rubbed fenders with Waltrip while fending him off.

Bonnett had no complaints about Waltrip's move, but another incident in the Twin 125s would raise questions. Baker had taken the lead from Bonnett with 11 laps to go in the second race. On lap 42, as a drizzling rain began to fall, NASCAR put out the yellow flag. During the race back to the flag, Waltrip tried to squeeze back in line and collided with Dale Earnhardt, who hit Bonnett and Ron Bouchard while fighting for control. Bonnett spun to the apron, finished seventh and blasted Waltrip: "He saw he was going to go from second to about sixth, so he turned right into Earnhardt to get back in line."

Allison led most of the first Twin 125, but on the last lap, Cale Yarborough and Terry Labonte

slingshotted past him in turn three. After finishing third, Allison said, "Maybe the strategy of the driver could be better, but I guess those things are going to happen." Allison clearly had one of the fastest cars, but it was not invincible. The rules had remained stable for almost a year, giving mechanics time to refine their cars. There was no runaway favorite.

Although Waltrip was the focus of prerace controversy, it took only four laps of the 500 for it to switch to Allison. As the leaders thundered through turn four, Allison's rear bumper fell off after a tap from Yarborough. The bumper skittered along the banking near the wall, momentarily out of harm's way, as more than half the field safely roared past. Finally, at the exit of turn four, the bumper slid back into the racing groove and passed under the right rear tire of the Pontiac driven by Joe Millikan, who was running about 25th. Millikan lost control and nosed headfirst into the outside wall. Four other cars became involved.

The accusations started even before the green flag came back out. Tim Brewer, Yarborough's crew chief, told CBS pit reporter Larry Nuber: "Cale said that Bobby and he touched, but I got a feeling that somewhere along the lines that bumper was intended to come off. And I don't know what manner it was fastened on the car but it wasn't fastened on there good enough to stay. . . That's wanting it an awful lot to want to win that way."

Gary Nelson, Allison's crew chief, responded: "No way. That's a very dangerous situation. I wouldn't risk anybody's life that way."

When the race resumed, the lead pack organized itself into a freight train of some 20 cars, with Allison, Earnhardt and Harry Gant trading the lead. Earnhardt seemed the strongest. He was the only one who could flat-foot it all the way around. Parsons, the pole winner, never led a lap. Alone, his car had been fine. In traffic, it was a squirrel.

Earnhardt had just taken the lead from Allison on lap 35 when he slowed and silently coasted to the pits. He was out of gas. His engine then blew a head gasket, and Earnhardt retired after only 44 laps.

Now Allison's car emerged as the strongest. By lap 51, he had broken the draft and was 15 car lengths ahead of Joe Ruttman in second. Allison's lost bumper had not seriously impaired the handling or speed of his car, even though he had shed not only the bumper but a piece of the body, as Ruttman's in-car camera clearly showed.

By halfway, Allison had led 66 laps. On lap 105, as Allison led a dozen cars toward turn one, a slow-moving Buick driven by Bobby Wawak erupted in a cloud of engine smoke in front of the pack. Bonnett, riding second, let off the gas and waved his right arm to warn those behind him. The warning came too late for Labonte, who rammed Bonnett and turned him head-on into the outside wall. Some cars made it through the chain-reaction crash, others didn't. When the smoke cleared, Bonnett, Baker, Petty and Parsons were out of it, along with two others. Petty cracked a bone and tore ligaments in his right foot and left Halifax Hospital on crutches, although his father, Lee, quipped, "I think he'll be able to plow tomorrow."

OPPOSITE: By 1982, Bobby Allison was a graying veteran of 44. He came into the 1982 race with 18 previous 500s under his belt, and with two second-place finishes and a victory in his last four attempts.
BELOW: The most controversial moment of the race occurred on lap four. Joe Millikan loses control of his car and crashes an instant after running over Bobby Allison's bumper, which has fallen off his car. The bumper is visible in the upper image in the gray area of the asphalt near the wall.

Now only Waltrip seemed capable of challenging Allison. On lap 145, Waltrip moved to the outside of Allison in turns one and two. Ruttman, who never led a lap despite running in the lead pack all day, got behind Waltrip and they drafted past Allison. Waltrip was still leading six laps later when smoke poured from his exhaust pipes as he entered turn one. His engine had blown. Ruttman cracked the throttle to avoid hitting Waltrip as Allison roared back into the lead.

After the final pit stops, Allison ran the final 39 laps on a single tank of gas, gradually extending his lead to more than 20 seconds. Allison and his team took something of a gamble on gas mileage, but Nelson's calculations were correct. Allison's engine sputtered a moment before he took the checkered flag, but he crossed the line 22.87 seconds ahead of Cale Yarborough. His car promptly ran out of gas and coasted to a stop at the head of pit road. He needed an extra splash to drive to victory lane.

Afterward, the talk was not of gas but loose bumpers. Yarborough and Brewer were particularly suspicious because, as Brewer said, "We came down here a few weeks back (during testing) and found we could run faster, handle better and get better mileage from our fuel without out a rear bumper."

Allison said that NASCAR had made the team move the location of the bumper earlier in the week "and I guess we didn't get it back on good." The lack of a bumper made his car loose, not better, Allison said, and the team had to adjust the car to compensate. Allison dismissed the controversy that threatened to envelop his second 500 victory. He had suffered a galling defeat in 1981 and now it was time to recoup. "I knew right from the start I had the strongest car," he said. "I knew if nothing happened, the race was ours."

BELOW: Allison's second victory was almost as overwhelming as his first. He beat Cale Yarborough again, this time by more than 22 seconds. As Allison crawled out of his car in victory lane, CBS commentator Ned Jarrett moves in for an interview. Between them is Bill Brodrick of Union 76, who became a minor celebrity by appearing in victory lane every week.

1983

IN 1983, CREW CHIEF WADDELL WILSON CAME TO DAYTONA determined to give his driver, Cale Yarborough, the chance to top 200 mph. Speeds had been creeping slowly higher since 1978, and Benny Parsons had cracked 200 mph for the first time at Talladega in the spring of 1982. Wilson wanted his car to be the first over 200 mph at Daytona.

Wilson's cars had won four straight Daytona 500 poles, with Buddy Baker in 1979 and 1980, Bobby Allison in 1981 and Parsons in 1982. But in the first practice sessions, he couldn't figure out why Yarborough wasn't any faster than the other drivers.

"All the way through practice and right up to qualifying, I couldn't figure out why we weren't faster," Wilson recalls. "I had spent time in the wind tunnel, and the car was supposed to go 203. I worked and worked and worked, but I couldn't get it to go any faster. I couldn't sleep. In passing, Cale said, 'We're okay.' What I didn't know was that the son-of-a-gun was sandbagging!"

In qualifications, Yarborough mashed the throttle. And on the first lap, his orange-and-white No. 28 Hardee's Chevrolet Monte Carlo hit 200.503 mph. As the crowd buzzed over that news, Yarborough went into the third turn on his second lap and the Chevy went into a slow-motion slide. The car lifted off and did a reverse half flip onto its roof as it backed into the wall. It landed right-side up, its roof crushed, and spun to a stop. Yarborough emerged unhurt, saying, "It all got quiet except for the hum of the engine." Wilson consulted the team about repairing the badly damaged car. They were not up for it. So Wilson and Yarborough went to a year-old backup, a Pontiac Grand Prix, and forfeited the record-breaking pole run, as well as the record of a fifth straight pole for Ranier Racing. Ricky Rudd won the top starting spot at 198.864 mph.

The Twin 125s were loaded with action—and trouble. Dale Earnhardt won the first of his record twelve Twin 125 victories with a last-lap pass of A. J. Foyt. On the sixth lap, Bruce Jacobi received permanent head injuries when his car flipped violently through the backstretch grass. Jacobi died four years later. The second race also was settled with a last-lap pass. Neil Bonnett swung around Richard Petty and nipped him by half a car length. The second race also had a violent backstretch crash, but

Rusty Wallace was not seriously hurt after flipping his car through the puddles and mud.

Yarborough would have been the clear favorite with his primary car, but in his backup, he was just one of many fast drivers. In the first eight laps, there were five different leaders and six lead changes. Geoff Bodine was strong. Richard and Kyle Petty ran one-two for a while and traded the lead once. Father led 29 laps, son led nine, but both blew their engines before the halfway point.

CBS had movable cameras and audio hookups in the cars of Yarborough and Tim Richmond, but Richmond was gone after 24 laps with a blown engine. Yarborough, however, gave television viewers the most intimate ride ever in a 500 telecast. CBS announcer Ken Squier chatted with Yarborough during the six caution periods, often questioning him at length.

On lap 63, the in-car camera showed Yarborough take the lead from Dick Brooks with a classic slingshot pass on the backstretch. Moments later, as the lead pack crossed the start-finish line, fourth-place runner Earnhardt's engine blew up. He quickly pulled out of line as the yellow flag flew. In the race back to the flag, Dick Brooks slowed for Lake Speed. Darrell Waltrip, coming at full speed, had to turn suddenly to avoid Brooks. Waltrip spun, crashed into the inside wall and shot across the track into the outside wall. He suffered a concussion and spent the night in the hospital.

As the race wore on, the lead continued to change every few laps. By the time it was over, it was one of the most competitive Daytona 500s ever, with 59 lead changes among 11 drivers. Bill Elliott led a few laps. Joe Ruttman had one of the strongest cars and led 16 times for 57 laps—the most of anyone. Yarborough led here and there, but mostly laid back. "I'm just biding my time," he told Squier.

In the final 15 laps, Baker and Yarborough sparred at the front. Baker took the lead on lap 189. And there he remained as the final laps were run, leading a four-car pack that included Yarborough, Ruttman and Elliott. Once again, the race came down to the last lap.

As the leaders came off turn two, Baker moved down to protect the inside, but he didn't move down far enough. Yarborough breezed by, followed by Ruttman. In turn three, Ruttman drifted high and Baker moved below him. Yarborough was home free as Baker and Ruttman battled. From behind them, in the final few hundred yards, Elliott moved to the outside and nipped them both at the line. Baker was third, Ruttman fourth.

A national television audience rode with Yarborough past the checkered flag and through the cooldown lap. "I knew what I had to do, Ken," Yarborough said. "It's like a checkers game, you know. You put yourself in the right spot and you can win the game."

BELOW: After completing 36 laps, Bosco Lowe came to the pits. He lost control on pit road, spun and hit the pit wall and a loose tire, which went flying. No one was injured in the close call.

LEFT: Driving his back-up Pontiac after crashing in qualifications, Cale Yarborough leads the pack through the tri-oval on his way to his third Daytona 500 victory. Trailing are Geoff Bodine, Buddy Baker, Bobby Allison, Dick Brooks and others.

1984

BY 1984, DARRELL WALTRIP HAD DEVELOPED HIS OWN KING-SIZED JINX with the Daytona 500. Unlike Buddy Baker, who had come close time and time again before winning, Waltrip couldn't seem to do anything right in the big race.

Waltrip entered NASCAR in 1972 and raced in his first 500 in 1973, finishing a credible 12th. But by 1984, after 11 starts in the 500, Waltrip had led only 22 laps. By then, he was arguably the sport's biggest star, certainly its most controversial, given his outspokenness and aggressive driving.

Waltrip had won 57 races by 1984, as well as two Winston Cup championships. He had won Twin 125 qualifying races in 1976, 1978, 1979 and 1981. But in the 500 itself, more often than not, Waltrip's car was junk. His best result had come in 1979, when he finished second to Richard Petty after the Cale Yarborough-Donnie Allison last-lap crash.

One of Petty's most vivid memories of that victory was the sight of Waltrip in his rear-view mirror on the cool-down lap, bouncing up and down and waving his arms with excitement and glee after finishing second. As it turned out, that was the last good Daytona 500 Waltrip would have for quite some time. He blew his engine in each of the next three Daytona 500s, and had one of the worst crashes of his career in the 1983 race, suffering a concussion that left him addled for several weeks.

The man who still had his finger on the pulse of Daytona power was Waddell Wilson. In 1984, Wilson and his driver, Cale Yarborough, had unfinished business. And on pole day, Yarborough officially became the first driver to qualify for the Daytona 500 at more than 200 mph. He reached 201.848 mph and, unlike 1983, did not crash. It was Yarborough's fourth Daytona 500 pole.

Yarborough won the first Twin 125 after Buddy Baker failed to outfox the cagey veteran. Baker was leading with eight laps to go, but decided he would not be a sitting duck. Baker slowed and forced Yarborough to pass. Yarborough took off and Baker could not catch him. Yarborough won by 1.8 seconds. In the second race, Bobby Allison held off Harry Gant. Waltrip struggled to a 13th-place finish.

It was in 1984 that the fourth turn was dubbed "Calamity Corner" after three vicious wrecks. Ricky Rudd was battered and bruised in a wild, tumbling, sidewinding crash in the Busch Clash, but he won two weeks later in Richmond. In the second Twin 125, Randy LaJoie spun off turn four. His car began flying and went underside-first into the inside wall before flipping end over end to a hard stop. The next day, in a consolation race, a car ricocheted off the inside wall into the path of another car. Both cars exploded in flames. Fortunately, none of the drivers was seriously injured.

The drivers expressed their concern by staging a safe 500, which had no serious incidents. President Ronald Reagan gave the command, "Gentlemen, start your engines!" by phone from the White House. Yarborough, Allison, Earnhardt and Petty took turns leading the early laps of the race, but Petty and Allison fell out early with mechanical problems. Yarborough clearly had the strongest car, leading 51 of the first 100 laps. Yarborough's car was so fast, he twice passed leading cars on the outside in the third turn.

Yarborough led most of the second half of the race, but Earnhardt and Terry Labonte were also strong, as well as Bill Elliott and Waltrip, who led for the first time on lap 142. Waltrip took the lead again on lap 162 during green flag pit stops. The race's final caution period came at lap 177, but four leaders—Waltrip, Yarborough, Labonte and Earnhardt—decided to remain on the track and hold their positions.

After the race resumed on lap 183, six cars pulled away from the field. And as the final lap started, it was Waltrip, Yarborough, Earnhardt, Neil Bonnett, Harry Gant and Bill Elliott. For 38 laps, Waltrip had grimly hung onto the point. But he knew how fast Yarborough was. "I knew what was going to happen and I didn't see no need of getting worried about it," Waltrip said afterward. "On the last lap, I was thinking second."

Yarborough made his move on the backstretch—the same move that had failed spectacularly in 1979 against Donnie Allison but worked perfectly in 1983 against Baker. Waltrip moved to the middle of the track, but did not aggressively block. Yarborough made the pass without drafting help.

Earnhardt also moved on Waltrip, but didn't begin his pass until turn four. He nipped Waltrip at the line, while Bonnett held off Elliott for fourth. Yarborough won by eight car lengths. For the sixth time in his career, Yarborough had a chance to make a last-lap pass for victory in a NASCAR race. For the sixth time, he did it. And for the first time since Fireball Roberts in 1962, a single driver had won the pole, his qualifying race and the 500.

Yarborough's fourth Daytona 500 victory was his most dominating performance. "I didn't see a car out there all day that I couldn't pass when I wanted to," he said. "I wanted to be in second place until the last lap. Once I got it, I held onto it until it was time to make my move."

For Waltrip, it was another disappointing finish. But he was not complaining. He said, "They had to carry me out of here on a stretcher last year, so I'm happy."

OPPOSITE: Honorary Starter William Howard of Piedmont Air Lines gives the field the green flag for the 26th annual Daytona 500. Forty-two cars started the race. BELOW: Cale Yarborough takes the checkered flag to win his second consecutive 500. About eight car lengths behind him, beyond the view of this image, Dale Earnhardt is edging past Darrell Waltrip to take second place.

1985

AS THE GARAGES OPENED FOR 1985 SPEEDWEEKS, stock car fans were captivated by the growing success of NASCAR's "Huck Finn," a young man with a thick Georgia drawl and bushy, red hair named Bill Elliott. Most of the Winston Cup series races were now televised, and fans around the country had agonized with Elliott in 1982 and 1983 as he struggled to win his first race.

Elliott was 20 when he and his brothers first brought the family's race car to the Winston Cup tracks in 1976. The Elliotts served a long apprenticeship. It took them three years to post a top-five finish. Elliott's first Daytona 500 was in 1978. He finished eighth, and turned a few heads.

Elliott finished sixth in the 1981 race, and fifth in 1982. In 1983, he drafted with Cale Yarborough on the last lap to pass Buddy Baker and finish second. It was a position that Elliott would come to know well. He lost by half a car length to Richard Petty at Rockingham less than a month after the 1983 500. He finished second in the Southern 500. Finally, in the season's final race at Riverside, Elliott broke through with his first victory.

In 1984, after running fifth in the 500, Elliott scored victories at Michigan, Charlotte and Rockingham, where he nipped Harry Gant at the finish line by a foot. He finished third in the Winston Cup championship and was voted NASCAR's most popular driver.

When testing for the 1985 Daytona 500 got underway, Elliott was a half-second faster than anyone else. In the run for the pole, Elliott shattered Yarborough's year-old record, reaching 205.114 mph. Yarborough was second fastest at 203.814 mph. "I guess I was pretty close to what they call the ragged edge," Elliott said afterward. "It's unbelievable, but at times it felt out of aerodynamic control. At that point, I was just riding it. I wasn't driving it."

BELOW: After grabbing the lead on lap 192, Neil Bonnett led until his engine blew in the tri-oval three laps later. As Bonnett spun through the grass toward the first turn, Elliott jumped into the lead. After the caution period for Bonnett's spin, Elliott breezed in a final one-lap sprint to the checkered flag.

In the first Twin 125, Elliott was more dominant than ever, leading 48 of the 50 laps. Second-place Darrell Waltrip finished 38 seconds behind. "Boys, the handwriting is on the wall," Waltrip said. Yarborough won the second race, which was a much closer affair. He passed David Pearson in the first turn of the last lap and won by two car lengths. The second race marked the first big-league start for Bobby Allison's son, Davey, who dropped out after one lap with a broken clutch and failed to qualify for the 500.

On the eve of the race, Elliott admitted, "I guess we have been impressive. It's sure a long way from when we came here in 1977, ran 170 and didn't make the field, isn't it?" In the race, Yarborough grabbed the lead from Elliott on lap three. Yarborough sensed that his car was equal to Elliott's. And he led three times for a total of 32 laps in the early going. But on lap 62, his engine failed.

Most of the race was run under the green flag, and Elliott at times stretched his lead to 25 seconds or more. The terrific pace took an unusually high toll of cars. Tim Richmond crashed on lap 67. Petty lost his clutch. From lap 82 to 98, Bobby Allison, Dale Earnhardt, Benny Parsons, A. J. Foyt and David Pearson all blew their engines. Terry Labonte and Harry Gant also lost engines.

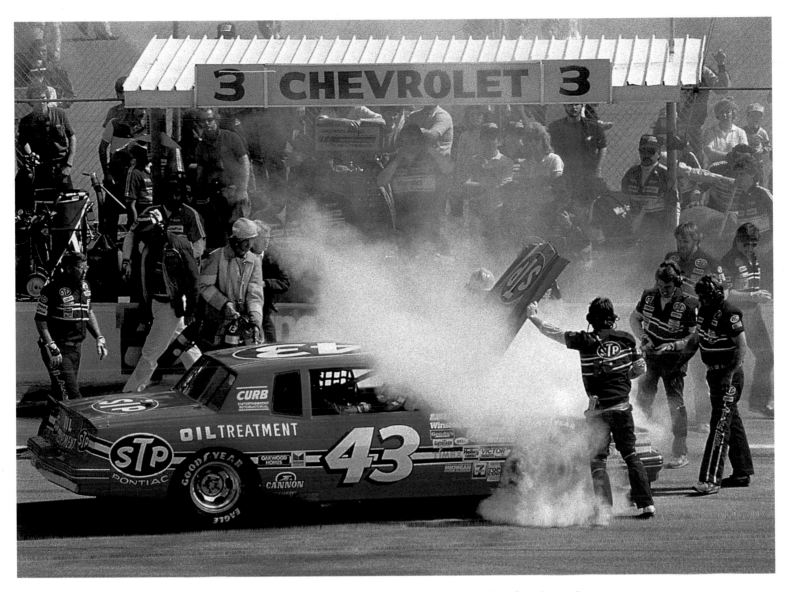

On lap 160, Elliott was ahead by 26.5 seconds and running away with the race. But four late yellow flags, which fell on laps 162, 174, 192 and 197, bunched the field and kept Elliott from getting away. Neil Bonnett posed the greatest threat to Elliott, leading from laps 166 through 173, and again on laps 192 through 194. But with five laps to go, Bonnett's engine blew and he spun to a stop in the tri-oval grass.

The final caution period led to a one-lap shootout for the victory, but Elliott's only remaining challenger, and the only other driver on the lead lap, was journeyman Lake Speed. Elliott had an easy final trip around the oval and flashed under the checkered flag almost a full second ahead of Speed.

"Ten years ago, when I started racing. . . if they had told me I'd win this race and this much money ($185,500), why, I would have told them that they weren't nothin' but a big ol' liar," Elliott said. "Now that we've won it, it feels just as good as me and all of us imagined it would back in '77. It's beyond words how happy I feel right now. This is the race. And if I never win another one, I'll always have this."

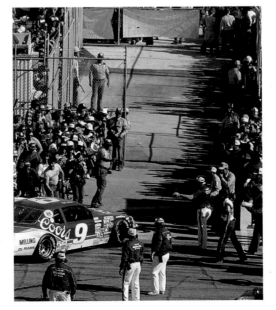

ABOVE: Richard Petty's car goes up in smoke on pit road. Petty led two laps, but retired after 80 laps because of clutch failure. He finished 34th.
LEFT: Less than three hours after the green flag fell, Elliott turned left into Daytona's Victory Lane. He had averaged 172.265 mph and led 136 of the 200 laps. He went on to win 11 races in 1985, but finished second in the Winston Cup championship to Darrell Waltrip.

1986

AN ERA WAS ENDING WHEN BILL ELLIOTT WON the 1985 Daytona 500. The 14 Daytona 500s preceding the 1985 race had been won by Richard Petty, Cale Yarborough, Bobby Allison, Buddy Baker, David Pearson, Benny Parsons or A. J. Foyt.

All of these drivers except Pearson were still racing in 1986, but most were finished winning. Baker's final victory came in 1983. Petty saw victory lane for the last time in 1984. Yarborough would keep running until 1988, but his final victory, as it turned out, had come at Charlotte in October 1985. Pearson's last victory was in 1980, and he made the 1985 Daytona 500 his last.

The old warhorses were being supplanted by new lions, including Elliott, Dale Earnhardt, Terry Labonte, Mark Martin, Rusty Wallace and Geoff Bodine, a hard-charging hotshoe from the northern modified ranks. As a teenager in the 1960s, Bodine took home movies of the 500 from the back of the family station wagon parked inside turn four.

Bodine led six laps as a Daytona rookie in 1979 before his engine blew. In 1983, he qualified second. And in the 1984 and 1985 500s, driving for the ever-stronger Hendrick Motorsports team, Bodine had finished eighth and seventh. Along the way, he had won three races. Although Bodine had endured a winless 1985, he had a new crew chief, Gary Nelson, who had guided Bobby Allison to his only Winston Cup championship in 1983. Nelson had a special knack for Daytona. Allison won the 1982 Daytona 500 with Nelson as crew chief. The previous July, lightly regarded Greg Sacks had won the Firecracker 400 in a DiGard research and development car prepared by Nelson.

Elliott once again won the pole, this time with a speed of 205.039 mph, which was just a fraction slower than his record-setting 1985 speed. But Elliott had no monopoly on speed in 1986. Chevrolet debuted a new, sleeker Chevrolet Monte Carlo and Bodine drove one to the second fastest speed at 204.545 mph. He decided to run the same car in the Busch Clash, and had a close call when he spun, but didn't hit anything. NASCAR President Bill France Jr. dropped by Bodine's garage and called him, "Mr. Lucky."

RIGHT: Geoff Bodine dominated the race after a big crash in turn four, but for most of that time, Dale Earnhardt was on his bumper. While Earnhardt led 10 laps after the crash, Bodine was in front for 65 circuits.

Twenty-six drivers qualified above 200 mph, but rain washed out two practice days, so there was more tension than usual before the Twin 125s. But the races were run without serious trouble. Allison led most of the first race, but Elliott passed him in the first turn of the last lap and won by two car lengths. Dale Earnhardt won the second race by two seconds over Bodine.

"It's going to be an interesting 500," Bodine said. "No one's going to run away like Bill did last year. Earnhardt and Elliott are strong, and I think we're next in line. But Allison ran great, Darrell Waltrip came on strong and Terry Labonte is running good."

As the race got underway, Bodine and Earnhardt dominated the early going, but Neil Bonnett, driving Junior Johnson's Chevy, was also fast, leading laps 43 through 74 before suddenly falling back on a restart with transmission problems. Richard Petty battled a loose car until lap 63, when he smacked the wall and suffered a shoulder injury.

Petty's crash sparked a spate of yellow flags for mostly minor incidents that ate up 41 laps between laps 65 and 128. The biggest incident occurred on lap 117 when Bonnett, already many laps down, broke a wheel in turn three and spun in front of the pack. Eleven cars became involved, including those driven by Yarborough, Joe Ruttman, Buddy Baker and Elliott.

The final 70 laps were run under the green flag, and by then Bodine and Earnhardt had made it a two-car race. Bodine was in front at lap 150, but Earnhardt sat on his bumper, shifting his car back

ABOVE: Geoff Bodine celebrates in Victory Lane with his wife, Kathy, and the Unocal race queens. "It was a relief when I saw Earnhardt pull down and go onto pit road," Bodine said. "I had a plan for how I was going to win. But he did too. It would have been a very exciting last lap, but it was a lap no one ever saw."

and forth, messing with Bodine's psyche by making his car loose. Bodine pitted on lap 159, took fuel and right-side tires, and was out in 15.2 seconds. Earnhardt came in on the next lap and received the same service, but the gas man apparently didn't get all the gas in and Earnhardt briefly stalled the engine. The stop took 19.6 seconds. As the two leaders got back up to speed, Bodine's lead was almost the length of the backstretch.

Earnhardt, with drafting help from Parsons, began reeling in Bodine, who wasn't handling quite as well as he would have with four fresh tires. By lap 174, Earnhardt was only a second behind. Two laps later, Earnhardt moved up to Bodine's bumper. Bodine slowed to let him pass, but Earnhardt was content to wait. Earnhardt said afterward, "I was sitting there waiting, just saving tires and gas. I was gonna race him on the last lap. I was where I wanted to be."

But with three laps to go, Earnhardt slowed coming off turn four. He threaded his way between lapped cars in a frantic rush to the pits. "He's out of gas!" Bodine shouted to his crew on the radio. Earnhardt slid past his pit with a dead engine. It took a splash of fuel and a shot of ether to get the car restarted. The engine refired, but it was sour. It had burned a piston. Earnhardt was done.

Bodine cruised the final three laps, relieved that he would not face a last-lap duel. "Then I got on the radio and said, 'Do we have enough gas?'" Bodine recalls. Nelson assured Bodine he had enough. Bodine won by 11.26 seconds over Labonte. In the coming two seasons, Bodine and Earnhardt would have many bitter, metal-bending battles, but fate and the lack of a gallon of gas ordained a quiet ending for this 500.

"My dreams and my goals were fulfilled on that day," Bodine said. "And it was pretty darn early in my career." Bodine's parents, Eli and Carol June, were selling their oldest son's souvenirs from a trailer across from the track. "After victory lane, the press box interview, the media and all the hoopla, I put my street clothes on and went down to the Kmart parking lot and signed autographs and helped sell souvenirs," Bodine recalls. "They never expected me down there, but that's what we did."

BELOW: On lap 116, Neil Bonnett's wheel broke and his car went out of control in a heavy pack of traffic. Eleven cars were caught up in the melee and several front-runners were knocked out of contention. Cars in this image were driven by Lake Speed (75), Harry Gant (33), Joe Ruttman (26), Cale Yarborough (28), Kyle Petty (7), and Bill Elliott (9).

1987

ALTHOUGH DAVEY ALLISON WAS CLASSIFIED A ROOKIE for the 1987 Daytona 500, he was hardly green at the speedway. The 25-year-old Allison had grown up with Speedweeks as he followed his famous father. Davey was 16 when Bobby Allison won his first 500 in 1982.

Davey had run in the Twin 125s in 1985 and again in 1986, failing both times to qualify for the 500. But in 1987, Allison arrived with a potent, if untested, team. At the end of 1986, car owner Harry Ranier had split with Cale Yarborough, crew chief Waddell Wilson and sponsor Hardee's. As replacements for the No. 28 Ford, Ranier assembled Allison, crew chief Joey Knuckles, engine builder Robert Yates and sponsorship from Texaco, establishing the roots for one of NASCAR's most memorable and beloved teams.

Bill Elliott thrust himself back in the forefront with a victory in the Busch Clash. Elliott followed on a rain-delayed Monday pole qualifying session with a record-setting lap of 210.364 mph, shattering his own 1985 mark by more than 5 mph. It took Elliott only 42.783 seconds to make his way around the 2.5-mile oval. It stands today as the fastest lap ever run at Daytona in a stock car. NASCAR in 1987 had a new rule limiting qualifying to one lap, and Elliott said, "One lap at that pace around here is all a man can stand."

The redesigned Ford Thunderbirds had the edge in speed in 1987, and young Allison alternated with Elliott as the fastest in practice. Davey qualified second at 209.084 mph. Bobby Allison also was fast, and started side by side with his son in the front row of the second Twin 125.

But the handling on Davey's car was less than ideal, providing the race's most exciting moment. As he went for the lead in turn one on lap 39, Allison lost the back end of his car. As the car began to spin, he let off the gas and gathered it up. It slid down on the apron, then tried to spin again back up the track, but Allison deftly caught it again. He recovered to finish sixth. Benny Parsons, substituting for a pneumonia-stricken Tim Richmond, won the race. Bobby Allison was second.

Elliott was supposed to run away with the first race, but he barely led at all. Buddy Baker led most of the early laps. During a round of pit stops on lap 21, Ken Schrader, driving for Junie Donlavey, darted back out in the lead after his crew decided to add fuel only. Elliott played a waiting game, but on the last lap, Schrader would not yield the inside. Schrader forced the stronger Elliott to the outside, and they came out of the fourth turn side by side. Elliott edged ahead, but then Schrader's momentum in the lower groove carried him ahead. Schrader won by a few inches.

It was Schrader's first victory in Winston Cup racing, and a heartwarming win for the 62-year-old Donlavey, who had been fielding cars since 1950, and was one of the most popular and well-liked owners in the garage. Donlavey was slow reaching victory lane because he was interrupted so often on his way there by his many friends and well-wishers.

The preliminary races had a number of crashes, but the 500 was crash-free for the third time, although four yellow flags briefly slowed the action. Elliott led the first 35 laps but lost his edge, and others took over at the front, including Baker and Schrader.

As for the Allisons, neither was a factor. Bobby finished sixth. Davey was 27th, 16 laps down, hampered by a variety of problems. Neither led a lap. Meanwhile, Elliott's team kept making adjustments to his car, and as the race wore on, his car again emerged as the one to beat.

With 40 laps to go, Earnhardt was leading. But on lap 166, a resurgent Baker pushed his

OPPOSITE: Bill Elliott leads a group of cars toward the first turn in the 1987 race. Elliott led 104 of the 200 laps, but did not dominate quite as completely as he had in 1985. But his Ford became stronger as the race wore on, and was invincible when Geoff Bodine sputtered to the pits, out of gas, with three laps to go. **BELOW:** Bill Elliott's crew changes four tires and adds 22 gallons of gasoline during a pit stop in the 500. Twice during caution periods, they got Elliott back out before the other frontrunners, allowing him to maintain the lead.

Oldsmobile in front and led for six laps. It was the last time Baker led the Daytona 500. As Earnhardt and Baker jostled for position, Elliott blew past both of them on lap 172 and retook the lead.

The fast pace and the timing of the caution periods set up a stretch run that included a series of swift, gas-only pit stops. They began on lap 185 with Elliott, whose stop took 6.3 seconds. Earnhardt took 9.9 seconds. One by one they came in, until only defending champion Geoff Bodine was left on the track. Bodine had run a strong race, but crew chief Gary Nelson knew that his only chance was to try to go all the way without refueling.

"We couldn't outrun Elliott, so we had to try to outlast him," Bodine said afterward. Three laps from the finish, Bodine's car ran out of fuel, just as Earnhardt's car had done the year before. But Bodine's engine died just past the point where he could have ducked into the pits, and he had to coast around the track. He finished 14th, one lap down.

Elliott led the final three laps as a pair of old veterans, Benny Parsons and Richard Petty, bore down on him. Elliott took the checkered flag about 10 car lengths in front of Parsons. Petty was third, followed by Baker and Earnhardt. Said Parsons, "There were times during the day when I thought Elliott was not invincible. Turned out in the end he wasn't."

For Elliott, superstardom was wearing thin, but not the joy of racing. "I admit it gets you tired, burns you down over that span of time with people seeming to pull from every direction," he said. "But all it takes to get you pumped back up is to get in a race car with a chance of winning."

OPPOSITE: Bill Elliott pulls off his helmet following a run at Daytona in 1987. He won the pole with a speed of 210.364 mph, circling the 2.5-mile track in just under 43 seconds. It is a record that still stands.
BELOW: Coming off the fourth turn during the 500, Elliott leads Geoff Bodine and Richard Petty as others follow. All three drivers led during the final 10 laps, but Elliott was in front for the checkered flag.

...T ABOUT everything there was to win in the NASCAR Winston Cup series except the Daytona 500.

At 41, Waltrip was beginning his 17th year in big-league stock car racing. He had burst onto the scene in the mid-1970s, winning 26 races for DiGard between 1975 and 1980. Waltrip moved on to Junior Johnson's team in 1981, and in the next six seasons became NASCAR's most dominant driver, winning another 43 races as well as three Winston Cup championships.

Waltrip never had as good a record at Daytona, but in the mid-1980s he at least gained a measure of consistency in the 500, finishing third in 1984 after leading 39 laps (his most ever to that point), third in 1985 and third again in 1986.

In 1987, after moving to Hendrick Motorsports and aligning with superstar crew chief Waddell Wilson, Waltrip had predicted victory in the 500. He led only one lap and finished eighth. The partnership with Wilson never got off the ground. So here was Waltrip in 1988, with Jeff Hammond as his new crew chief, once again predicting victory. "This is the team to beat," he said.

The pole position, however, went to Waltrip's teammate, Ken Schrader, at 193.823 mph. Davey Allison qualified second at 193.311 mph. Speeds were down drastically after NASCAR ordered the teams to install carburetor restrictor plates with one-inch openings at the superspeedways in the wake of a horrendous crash at Talladega in 1987 in which Bobby Allison tore out a section of trackside fencing, injuring several fans.

Bobby was 50 now, but exhibited no signs of slowing. He was fifth fastest in qualifications. In the first Twin 125, Allison took the lead on lap 20 and led the rest of the way, winning by four car lengths over Rusty

OPPOSITE: Pole winner Ken Schrader, with Davey Allison to his outside, takes the green flag to start the 30th Daytona 500.
LEFT: Bobby Allison's No. 12 Miller Buick, owned by brothers Mickey and Billy Stavola, was a powerful force throughout 1988 Speedweeks. Allison finished third in the Busch Clash, won his Twin 125 qualifying race and captured his third 500 trophy.
BELOW: Thirty-seven of the 42 cars in the 1988 race are visible in this panoramic view taken from above the fourth turn. Lap five has just begun as Darrell Waltrip leads the field in a mostly single-file line that stretches back into the fourth turn.
FOLLOWING PAGES: One of the most spectacular crashes in Daytona history occurred on lap 106 when Richard Petty lost control after a brush with Phil Barkdoll coming off turn four. Petty's car tumbled down the fence, then landed on its wheels and was T-boned by Brett Bodine's car. Petty was not seriously injured. The yellow flag flew for 21 laps while workers cleaned up the mess and fixed the retaining fence.

RIGHT: Twenty cars are visible in this image from the roof of the new Winston Tower.

Wallace. It was Allison's fifth victory in the 125s, and he also won the Goody's 300 Grand National series race two days later.

In the second Twin 125, Waltrip lived up to his boast, leading all 50 laps before winning by four car lengths over Dale Earnhardt. It was also Waltrip's fifth 125 victory—his first since 1981. At one point in the second race, Cale Yarborough made a stab at Waltrip, but spun out, triggering a 10-car crash.

With the drop of the green flag in the 500, Bobby Allison charged into the lead on the backstretch and led lap one, but Waltrip led lap two. These two drivers dominated the first half of the race. Allison led 36 consecutive laps beginning at lap 50. Waltrip took over on lap 86 and led the next 22 laps.

On lap 106, Richard Petty took his wildest ride at Daytona. It was not Petty's worst crash, but it instantly became his best known. As Petty told David Letterman a few days afterward, "There was more people watching this wreck than probably any wreck I've ever been in."

It started when Petty lost control coming out of turn four, possibly after a tap from Phil Barkdoll. Petty's car slid sideways for perhaps 100 feet until Barkdoll hit him in the left rear and A. J. Foyt struck his left front fender. Petty's car lifted off the ground, rear-end first. Barkdoll's car literally slid under Petty's rear end as it rose into the air. Petty's car did a reverse half-flip, then slammed down on its roof and began tumbling. Petty gripped the steering wheel and remained conscious as the car rolled violently four times, with its rear end on the retaining fence. Shedding parts in all directions, it flipped a fifth time and finally came down on its wheels, two of which were missing.

Petty's car twirled to a stop but was hit in the front by Brett Bodine, sending the wrecked hulk spinning like a top for four complete 360-degree turns before finally stopping again below the spectacular new Winston Tower being built above the start-finish line.

"Richard, are you all right?" radioed crew chief Dale Inman.

Petty fumbled for the switch and finally gasped, "I'll talk to you as quick as I get my breath." Petty banged up his ankle and had a few bruises, but was otherwise unhurt.

After Petty's crash, the fierce battle continued up front. When Waltrip took first on lap 164 and opened up a big lead over Bobby Allison, he appeared to be the driver to beat. But just after Waltrip made a fast fuel-only stop under the green flag, Harry Gant crashed on lap 175 and the field was shuffled during the ensuing caution period. When the race resumed with 18 laps to go, Parsons was in front, followed by Davey Allison, Waltrip and Bobby Allison.

As the field thundered through turn two, Waltrip dipped below Davey, who was stuck behind Parsons. As Waltrip passed Parsons, Bobby Allison went under Waltrip. Bobby and Darrell battled side by side for nearly an entire lap until Davey finally pushed his father ahead on the backstretch on lap 184 and popped in second himself.

Less than one lap later, Waltrip began falling back. His engine began skipping. He had led 69 laps, but his best chance yet for a 500 victory was over. Afterward, he said, "It was really tough out there those last 10 laps watching people I'd beaten all day pass me."

The Allisons, father and son, led the rest of the way. Davey never made a serious pass attempt on the last lap, although Bobby drifted high in turns three and four. Davey explained, "I went down low in three and four, but he was too strong."

At 50, Bobby Allison became the oldest 500 winner. And it was the first father-son, one-two finish in 500 history. It was not, however, the first in NASCAR history. Back in 1959 and 1960, Lee and Richard Petty had done it twice. The first time, at Lakewood Speedway in Atlanta in 1959, Lee had successfully protested when Richard was flagged the winner.

There was no such discord at Daytona. Said Bobby, "What a thrill, seeing Davey in my mirror and knowing we were going to sweep it."

BELOW: Bobby Allison speeds under the checkered flag to win the 1988 Daytona 500. Three car lengths back, just crossing the line, is his son, Davey. It was the first father-son, one-two finish in Daytona history.

1989

THE CHANGING OF THE GUARD IN NASCAR RACING was nearly complete as 1989 Speedweeks got underway. The stately Winston Tower loomed over the start-finish line and 8,000 new seats. Stock car racing was growing by leaps and bounds, and about to enter a new decade of even greater popularity.

On the track, some familiar old faces were gone for good. Cale Yarborough retired to become a team owner. Benny Parsons hung up his helmet to become a broadcaster. Buddy Baker retired (temporarily, as it turned out) after a blood clot formed in his head following a crash at Charlotte. And Bobby Allison's career ended suddenly when he was gravely injured at Pocono in June 1988.

The presence of the old stalwarts was missed, but new drivers quickly filled the void. Yarborough hired Dale Jarrett, who had started his first Daytona 500 start in 1988 at age 31. Jarrett completed all 200 laps and finished 16th. Another newcomer was Ernie Irvan, a 30-year-old hotshot from Salinas, Calif., who managed to snare the 33rd starting spot in 1989 for his first 500 start.

Ken Schrader, starting his second year at Hendrick Motorsports, was coming into his own. Schrader put his Chevy on the pole for the second straight year, lapping the speedway at 196.996 mph. His teammate, Darrell Waltrip, now one of the senior drivers in the Winston Cup series, qualified second. Schrader also won the Busch Clash. And he was just as dominant in the first Twin 125, leading 42 of the 50 laps before winning by a few car lengths over Morgan Shepherd. Fourteen cars crashed in the tri-oval on lap 18 after Rick Wilson and Lake Speed tangled.

Terry Labonte won the second Twin 125 by going nonstop while everyone else had to pit. Labonte won the caution-free event by 9.21 seconds over Sterling Marlin, who was emerging as one of swiftest of the new breed at Daytona. Labonte's average speed of 189.554 mph stands as the record for the Twin 125s.

The day before the 500, Waltrip won the Goody's 300 with a last-lap pass of Rusty Wallace. And as the 500 got underway before a record crowd of 140,000, Waltrip led the first 10 laps. But Schrader had the quickest car, and he passed Waltrip on lap 11 and went on to lead 39 of the first 100 laps of

RIGHT: Pit road swarms with activity during a round of pit stops under the yellow flag. This scene was common in 1989, as seven yellow flags slowed the race for 30 laps.
BELOW: The 1989 race was Dale Jarrett's second Daytona 500. It did not go well. Jarrett was able to return to the track after this fire in the infield, but he completed only 131 laps and finished 31st.

the race.

By halfway, Waltrip and his crew chief, Jeff Hammond, realized they were not going to outrun Schrader. In 1988, their car had been as "bad" as any on the big tracks, so Waltrip had named it "Betty" in honor of the Sawyer Brown hit *Betty's Bein' Bad*.

In 1989, however, "Betty" wasn't being quite as bad. So Hammond devised a fuel mileage strategy. In his years with Junior Johnson, Hammond had learned to be meticulous with gas mileage. Junior also had taught him to gamble for a fuel mileage victory whenever possible.

The final drama had its beginnings on lap 144, when Phil Barkdoll spun through the backstretch grass, hit the earthen berm next to Lake Lloyd and came to an unlikely finish with his car on its left side with its wheels off the ground. Everyone pitted. With 53 laps to go, Waltrip left pit road with a full tank of gas. Almost immediately, Hammond began imploring his driver to save gas.

Schrader jumped back into the lead on lap 155, followed by Dale Earnhardt. The two cars began to pull away. With 20 laps to go, they had a 7.2-second lead. By this time, Waltrip was drafting incessantly with other cars so he could crack the throttle as often as possible to save gas.

With about 25 miles to go, the cars began making gas-only pit stops. Schrader and Earnhardt came in on lap 190. Schrader left pit road 3.5 seconds behind Earnhardt, but quickly made up the lost ground and repassed him.

Two drivers, Waltrip and Alan Kulwicki, didn't stop. Kulwicki, running in his third 500, was leading. Waltrip clung to his bumper in a two-car draft. On lap 197, Kulwicki suddenly slowed with a tire problem. As he came to the pits for a replacement, Waltrip took the lead.

However, Waltrip, did not celebrate after Kulwicki's departure. His fuel pressure light began to flash. At about the same time, Schrader looked at the scoreboard and realized what his teammate was going to try to do. Schrader had led 114 laps, to no avail. "I realized. . . that Darrell was going to go

for it and we were in trouble," Schrader said afterward. "He had been legging it, and I knew that was his strategy—to gamble on going all the way without a last stop for gas."

As Schrader's heart sunk, Waltrip was in greater agony. At least twice in the last three laps, he was sure his gas tank was empty.

"It's out! It's gone! The fuel pressure is zero!" he shouted to Hammond on the radio. Then, "No, it's not! The fuel pressure has picked up! It's going again."

"Shake it, baby, shake it!" Hammond shouted to his driver, imploring him to steer the car back and forth to slosh any remaining fuel into the pickup.

"It's OK, now, I can make it," Waltrip said. "We might be able to. . . We'll try it."

There was no other choice, of course. And moments after sputtering across the finish line 7.64 seconds ahead of Schrader, Waltrip was again shouting on the radio. This time, however, it was, "I won the Daytona 500! I won the Daytona 500!"

In his 17th 500 start driving car number 17, Waltrip had finally won the only big trophy that had eluded him in his long career. Earnhardt, who finished third, said, "I'd sure like to see that gas tank." NASCAR inspectors said the same thing, but found nothing amiss when they looked. They also found almost no gas. One observer said, "For $5, I'd drink what was left."

ABOVE: Seventeen years of frustration was transformed into electrified joy for Darrell Waltrip when he pulled into Victory Lane after winning the 1989 race. To his right is his wife, Stevie, holding their daughter, Jessica, who was 17 months old.

1990

ABOVE: Actor Tom Cruise, playing the fictional driver Cole Trickle, is loaded onto a helicopter for a ride to the hospital in this scene from the filming of *Days of Thunder*.
BELOW: Derrike Cope celebrates in Victory Lane with two Unocal race queens. Cope established that his victory was no fluke when he won the Budweiser 500 at Dover Downs International Speedway on June 3, 1990.

THE MOST DISAPPOINTED DRIVER AT THE END of the 1989 Winston Cup season was Dale Earnhardt. With five races remaining in his quest to win a fifth championship, Earnhardt had led Rusty Wallace by 75 points. But bad breaks and a final-lap collision with Ricky Rudd at North Wilkesboro cost him dearly. Earnhardt won the final race at Atlanta, but lost the title to Wallace by 12 points.

Earnhardt stewed in his deer stand during the off-season. "The more I got to thinking about it, the madder I got," he said. "I'd shoot the ground just because I was mad."

His anger turned into determination, and Earnhardt returned to Daytona and quickly established his black No. 3 Goodwrench Chevrolet as one of the fastest cars. On pole day, he qualified second. Ken Schrader won the pole for the third straight year, reaching 196.515 mph in his Hendrick Chevrolet.

Earnhardt led the first 21 laps of his Twin 125 qualifying race, but fell back after a pit stop. He started 12th on a restart with 10 laps to go. Earnhardt passed 11 cars in eight laps. On lap 48, Earnhardt passed Dick Trickle, a short-track veteran from the Midwest, and took the lead for good. It was Earnhardt's third victory in the qualifying races.

In the first Twin 125, Geoff Bodine drove all 50 laps on a single tank of gas and won by 2.02 seconds over Harry Gant. Richard Petty led 15 laps in the middle of the race—the last laps he ever led at Daytona during Speedweeks.

A feisty Earnhardt mocked Bodine's victory. "If they run conservative in the 500 and worry about gas mileage, they're going to get their butts lapped," he said. The day before the 500, Earnhardt ran away with the Goody's 300 Grand National race. On race morning, the Daytona Beach *News-Journal's* Godwin Kelly reported that Earnhardt was so strong, he "could probably win on three wheels."

Earnhardt led 26 of the first 27 laps. By the halfway point, he had led 84 laps. Still, some drivers could stay with him. Geoff Bodine had a good car, as did Bill Elliott

and Terry Labonte. And Derrike Cope, a little-known driver with a good ride, surprised every-one with his tenacity.

Cope, 32, had started racing in his native Washington state. He first competed in Winston Cup in 1982. He had started two 500s, but failed to finish both. But he had landed the ride in Bob Whitcomb's Purolator Chevrolet for 1990. His crew chief was the skilled veteran Buddy Parrott. During Speedweeks, Cope was plagued by a throttle wiring problem, but Parrott had finally fixed it. After the final practice, Cope knew he had one of the strongest cars.

While Earnhardt dominated the race, Cope lurked in the background. He even led a couple of laps, and was still in the top five with 30 laps to go. By then, Earnhardt had a 27-second lead. After 11 starts—including a second, a third, a fourth and two fifths—Earnhardt was on the brink of win-ning his first Daytona 500 in dominating fashion.

On lap 193, Bodine spun in the first turn, causing a caution period. Everyone pitted except Cope, who took the lead. Parrott told his driver to go for broke on used tires. With only seven cars on the lead lap, the worst he could do was seventh.

On the restart with five laps to go, Earnhardt blew past Cope as the pack entered the third turn. Cope pulled in behind Earnhardt and managed to hold onto second, despite his used tires. As they started the final lap, Earnhardt, Cope, Labonte and Elliott had moved slightly ahead of the field.

On the backstretch, a piece of metal bell housing had tumbled to a stop on the asphalt. It came off Rick Wilson's car as his engine expired. In Earnhardt's motorhome, his wife, Teresa, watched on television. Now she rose to her feet and took their 14-month-old daughter, Taylor, in one arm. Her husband was on the backstretch. Cope made no moves. He had none to make.

Earnhardt drove over the bell housing and heard it hit the bottom of the car. Boom! The right rear tire blew up. Earnhardt held the wheel straight, let off the throttle and let his car climb the banking of turn three. He knew it was over for him.

ABOVE: Moments before the dramatic ending, Dale Earnhardt leads Derrike Cope and Rick Mast coming off the high banks. Cope was driving on used tires and using the entire track, but kept his throt-tle mashed to the floor.

OPPOSITE: An affectionate greeting from Dale Earnhardt usually came in the form of a pinch to the belly or a playful headlock. Although his 1990 Daytona 500 ended in bitter disappointment, he went on to win nine races that season and his fourth Winston Cup championship.

RIGHT: With Dale Earnhardt limping toward the line on a shredded tire, Derrike Cope flashes under the checkered flag to become one of the unlikeliest winners of the Daytona 500. Rick Mast trails in second, followed by Bill Elliott.

Cope, meanwhile, had been so loose on the last lap, he nearly hit the wall coming off turn two. But he kept the gas pedal mashed. He had vowed to himself to not let off, no matter what. He inched closer to Earnhardt on the backstretch. Suddenly, he saw Earnhardt's tire begin to lose its shape and elongate. Pieces of rubber flew off. The black car twitched sideways just a bit. Cope held a low line in turn three and rushed through the opening left by Earnhardt as he drifted up the banking.

From the grandstands, the incident happened so quickly and smoothly, it was as if it had been choreographed—like Earnhardt was giving way to Cope in a relay race. In the Earnhardt motorhome, Teresa was still bouncing Taylor Nicole up and down with excitement. A moment later, she stood in shock, and the baby started crying.

Cope looked in his rear-view mirror. Labonte was back there, but no threat. "I knew then that if I didn't lift anywhere, I had the race won," Cope said later. Pandemonium erupted in Cope's pit as he took the checkered flag. Whitcomb was so overcome, he had to sit on pit wall to catch his breath.

Earnhardt's crewmen had spilled onto pit road to bring him home. Now they climbed back over pit wall in stunned silence. Their driver finished sixth. It was no solace at that moment, but Earnhardt's skill in keeping his car under control in the third turn would quickly be recognized as one of the most memorable of his many remarkable displays of driving.

On the cool-down lap, Cope and Earnhardt experienced vastly different emotions. But they had the same thought. They had to rise to the occasion. Cope recalls, "I remember thinking to myself, 'Okay, Dad is telling you that when you get to victory lane, you better be on your best. Make sure the sponsors are taken care of. Make sure the hats are on.' All of that came rushing back to me." In victory lane, after saluting the crowd, the first thing Cope did was switch hats.

Earnhardt knew he had to face the cameras, too. He felt like crawling into a shell. But the last thing he wanted to be was a sore loser. He told himself: "You have to handle it just like Richard Petty would have done." The interview with David Hobbs of CBS was mercifully brief: "We run over some debris and cut a right rear tire down, David, uh, just a quarter lap from victory," Earnhardt said as he rubbed his ears with a wet cloth. He was still sitting in his car. "Not much you can do about it."

Indeed, there was little left to do but to carry home the only trophy that remained. After crewmen removed the wheel that still held the remains of the blown tire, car owner Richard Childress had it mounted and put on display in the museum at his shop in Welcome, N.C.

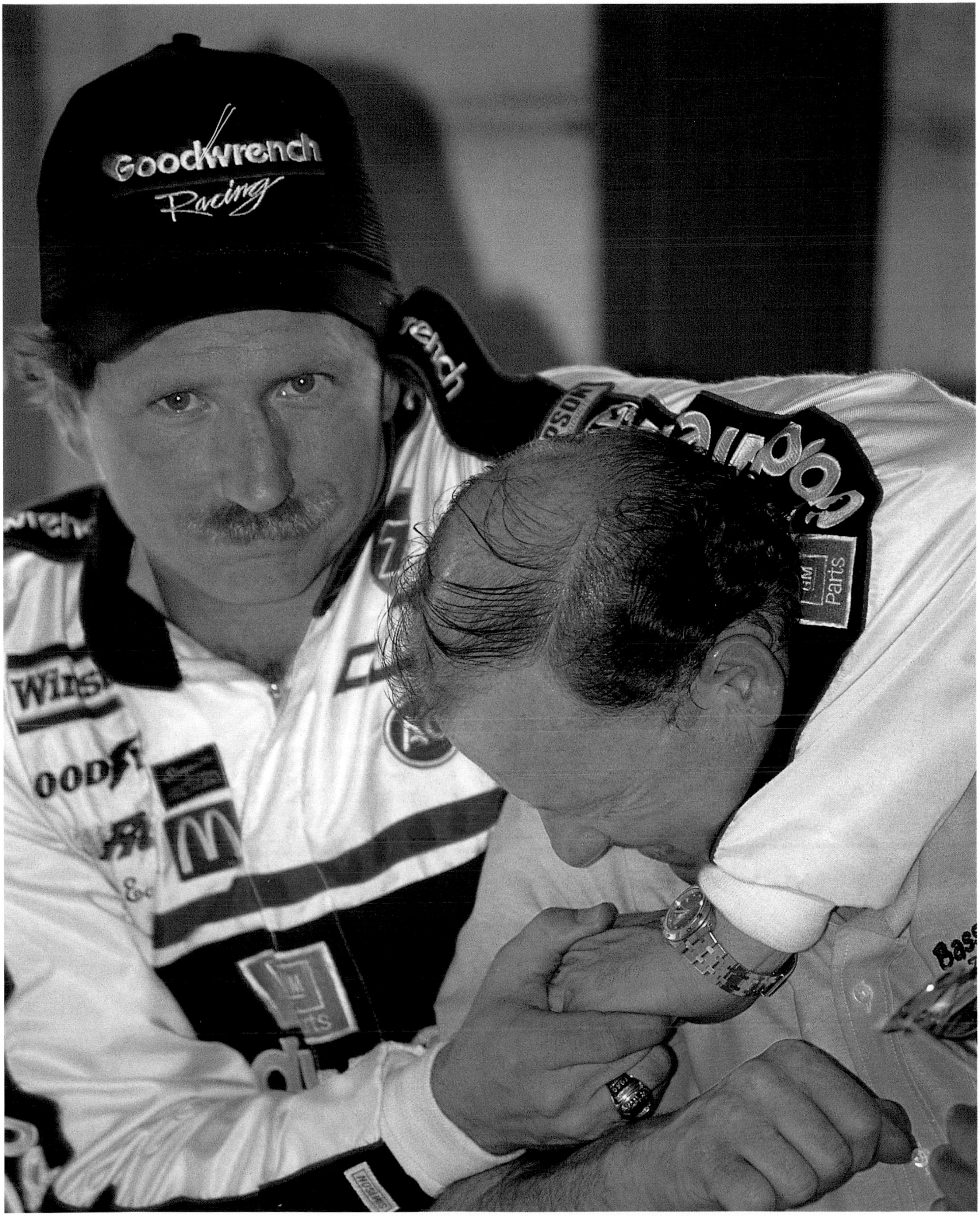
Goodwrench
Racing
Parts

1991

DALE EARNHARDT'S BITTER DEFEAT in the 1990 Daytona 500 did not dampen his enthusiasm in 1991. In the first race of Speedweeks, the Busch Clash, Earnhardt sliced through the entire field in a lap and a half and won easily. Once again, he was the favorite.

Davey Allison emerged as Earnhardt's strongest competition. Allison, with only four 500s under his belt, was driving like a seasoned veteran in his Robert Yates Racing Texaco Havoline Ford Thunderbird. Allison ran the fastest lap in the first practice, then won the pole at 195.955 mph.

Ernie Irvan, 32, a hard-charging fourth-year driver, qualified second. Irvan, like Derrike Cope, had come from the stock car tracks in the west. Irvan, driving the Morgan-McClure Kodak Chevrolet, won his first and the team's first Winston Cup race in 1990, but also gained a reputation for aggressive driving. Other drivers called him "Swervin' Irvan," and they blamed him for a crash at Darlington that left Neil Bonnett with a severe concussion.

Allison, meanwhile, said his confidence was "back to an all-time high" now that veteran Jake Elder was his crew chief. Elder was known for helping young drivers, but switched jobs so often his nickname was "Suitcase Jake." Allison was Elder's 21st driver.

Patriotism ran high at Daytona in 1991. In January, President George Bush launched Operation Desert Storm against Iraq. To honor the armed forces and help struggling teams, the R. J. Reynolds Tobacco Co. sponsored five cars, one for each branch of the military.

Allison and Earnhardt won the Twin 125s, but an ageless Richard Petty stole the spotlight, battling Hut Stricklin to the finish line to take second place by inches in the first race. Allison won the race, and as he watched the Petty-Stricklin battle develop in his rear-view mirror, he radioed to his crew, "Here comes the King!" Afterward, Petty was mobbed by the media and jubilant pit crew members. "Watch out!" he said. "We might be there."

Earnhardt won the first race despite a bump in the third turn of the final lap from Irvan, who finished second. Allison and Earnhardt had led every lap of their races and became co-favorites to win the 500. Allison vowed to "do whatever my fanny tells me to do" to win. Said Earnhardt, "We got our own game plan." Part of Earnhardt's plan was to win the Goody's 300 Grand National race, which he did handily, leading 90 of 120 laps. In the final Winston Cup "Happy Hour" practice, Earnhardt was so satisfied, he pulled in 30 minutes early.

OPPOSITE: As starter Harold Kinder waves the yellow and checkered flags simultaneously, Ernie Irvan wins the 500 driving on the apron of the track. Fearful that he would run out of gas, Irvan remained on the flat part of the track during most of the final lap.
ABOVE: Well before the start of the race, the field for the 1991 Daytona 500 is assembled on pit road. On the pole is the No. 28 Texaco Havoline Ford by virtue of Davey Allison's qualifying lap of 195.955 mph. Ernie Irvan's No. 4 Kodak Chevrolet sits in the second starting spot.

155

On race day, the media estimated that 145,000 fans watched as Earnhardt and Allison dominated early. Six incidents slowed the race in the first 81 laps, including a five-car melee on lap 31 after a fire broke out in Jimmy Spencer's car. Spencer, overcome by smoke, tumbled out of his car and rolled in the grass in front of the main grandstand. No one was injured in any of the accidents.

After lap 82, the race settled into 103 laps of green flag racing. The lead changed nine times as one leader after another headed to the pits for gas and tires. Allison led, then Sterling Marlin, then Rick Mast, Kyle Petty, Joe Ruttman, Irvan and Darrell Waltrip.

On lap 184, the yellow flag flew again when Richard Petty, a nonfactor in the race, smacked the wall. After Petty's car was towed to the garage, the race resumed on lap 189. Rusty Wallace had taken the lead during pit stops, but Earnhardt immediately muscled past. Kyle Petty tried to pass Wallace as well, but pinched Wallace into the outside wall coming off the fourth turn. Wallace spun and nailed Darrell Waltrip. Behind them, Derrike Cope, Hut Stricklin and Harry Gant also crashed.

The four-lap caution period that followed—the eighth of the day—set up the final duel. Earnhardt led. Irvan was now second. The green flag flew again on lap 194. At first, Earnhardt moved ahead by a few car lengths. But Irvan zeroed in on the black Chevrolet. Irvan's car was handling better. And in the first turn of lap 195, Irvan slipped under Earnhardt and eased into the lead.

Another 500 was slipping from his grasp, and Earnhardt battled with everything he had. But his car was loose. When Allison pulled alongside him coming off turn two on lap 197, Earnhardt lost control. He slammed into Allison, who hit the wall, then spun across the infield and hit the dirt embankment next to Lake Lloyd. Kyle Petty, who had led the most laps, also was involved.

Irvan, now leading, had his own problems as the race went under yellow. He was almost out of gas. On the last lap, he suddenly shouted into his radio: "I'll tell you what, this thing's running out of gas! We'll just make it back."

"Get it on the apron," ordered crew chief Tony Glover. That way, the last ounces of fuel could slosh from the tank into the fuel pickup. The engine sputtered for a moment in turn one. By turn three, it was fine. Irvan was home free.

Sterling Marlin, who led briefly on two occasions, finished second, followed by Ruttman and Mast. Earnhardt recovered from the crash to finish fifth. And that's what most irked Allison, who finished 15th. After a long cooling-off period in his transporter, Allison emerged holding his 13-month-old daughter, Krista Marie. He bounced her gently, as if to try to shake off his own frustration.

"He's just dad-gummed lucky," Allison said. "I cannot believe how lucky he is. When he gets involved in something, somehow he always manages to get out of it—to come out smelling like a rose."

The driver with a reputation for crashing avoided all the mayhem to win NASCAR's biggest race. "I think I won the one I needed to win," Irvan said. As for his nickname, "I like that name," Swervin' Irvan said. "It beats 'Bonehead,' which they named me one time."

BELOW, LEFT: Kyle Petty's crew fuels his car during the 1991 race. Petty started sixth and led 51 laps—the most of any driver—before being knocked out by the crash on the backstretch on lap 197.

BELOW, RIGHT: Another frantic minute has come to pit road at Daytona. Dale Earnhardt has already arrived and his crew is changing right-side tires, but most of the field is still coming in.

1992

FOR MANY NASCAR WINSTON CUP TEAMS, the first challenge of 1992 Speedweeks was passing inspection. During the off season, NASCAR President Bill France Jr. hired Gary Nelson, one of racing's savviest crew chiefs, to be the sanctioning body's technical director.

Nelson knew nearly every trick in the book, and he instituted exacting new inspection procedures. Nelson worked hard over the winter to acclimate the teams to his new ways, but most cars failed the prepractice inspection on Thursday, February 6. The garage lights burned until 6:30 p.m.

Many cars didn't fit body templates. Others had oversized fuel cells. On some, the air intake opening on the hood, known as the cowl, was too large. "The guys weren't that far out," Nelson said. "It was definitely a trying day, because I meant for the teams to have an easy time."

When the cars got onto the track, the Fords were fastest. It was not a matter of which car would win the pole, but which Ford. Sterling Marlin prevailed in Junior Johnson's Ford at 192.213 mph. Bill Elliott was second fastest in another Ford, followed by four more.

Davey Allison, who had come so close in 1991, crashed in practice the day before the Twin 125s. He recovered to finish third in the second qualifier behind Elliott and Morgan Shepherd. Dale Earnhardt won the first Twin 125 after tapping Marlin into a spin down the frontstretch while Marlin was leading.

Several crashes interrupted the races. One took out Richard Petty, who was preparing for his 32nd and final 500. Another took out Dale Jarrett, who was making his first start for Winston Cup's newest car owner, Joe Gibbs. Less than three weeks before, Gibbs had coached the Washington Redskins to a third Super Bowl victory. Gibbs watched the crash from the pits and lost no time adopting NASCAR jargon. It "was just one of those deals," he said.

By race eve, Earnhardt was again firmly in command, despite the Fords. He had won his third consecutive Goody's 300 as well as the International Race of Champions. In the IROC race, he had made another of his unforgettable racing moves, charging from third to first in the final few hundred yards. In final practice, Earnhardt once again ran only a few laps. "There's no reason to keep running it and wearing it out," he said. "I can't believe this week is going as good as it is."

ABOVE: During his 32nd and final Daytona 500, Richard Petty makes a pit stop. He started the race in 32nd, but finished 16th, two laps down.
BELOW: Thirty-year-old Davey Allison came to Speedweeks in 1992 with five Daytona 500s under his belt. He had finished second to his father in 1988 and won the pole In 1991. In 1992, he started sixth.

Petty was the grand marshal, and from his car he announced, "Okay, guys, let's go. Crank 'em up." Marlin and Elliott led the early laps. Allison took command on lap 56 and remained in front until a brief rain shower brought out the first yellow flag on lap 84. Earnhardt struggled with the handling of his Chevy and was not a factor.

The race restarted on lap 90. The race's key moment came two laps later on the backstretch when Elliott and Ernie Irvan both tried to pass Marlin, who was leading. Elliott went outside. Irvan went inside. Marlin was sandwiched. All three came together at the same time. Behind them, Allison backed off for a split second. Then he "moved outside, stood on the gas and went on as all hell broke loose right behind me."

Fourteen cars were involved in the crash, including nine of the 16 cars on the lead lap and nearly everyone who could have posed a threat to Allison. Besides Marlin, Elliott and Irvan, others involved included Jarrett, who was driving Gibbs' backup car, Earnhardt, Petty, Darrell Waltrip, Rusty Wallace and Ken Schrader.

Allison led most of the rest of the race. At the end, only lightly regarded Morgan Shepherd was left to contend with Allison. On the last lap, all Shepherd saw was Allison's bumper. Allison won by two car lengths. Geoff Bodine was third, followed by Alan Kulwicki. Earnhardt finished ninth. Petty was 16th, two laps down, in his final 500.

Until 1992, Petty and his father, Lee, had been the only father and son to win stock car racing's biggest race. Now the Allisons had done it, too. Bobby Allison joined his 30-year-old son in victory lane. "I'm very, very proud," the elder Allison said. "I keep saying it's really a special pleasure (when you) think about fathers around the country who would like to feel this way about their sons."

Davey's best finish in five previous 500s was second, when he followed his father across the line in 1988. Davey still ranked 1988 as the greater thrill, but agreed that the significance of his own 500 victory would soon sink in. He said, "Probably tomorrow morning, I'll be floating when I wake up."

OPPOSITE: Davey Allison chats with Rusty Wallace over the noise of engines in the Winston Cup garage. While Allison was destined for victory, Wallace found himself with another disappointing 500. He was involved in the crash on lap 92 and finished 31st, 50 laps down. **ABOVE:** As Davey Allison unleashes a torrent of pent-up champagne, crew members and Miss Winstons flinch and duck. Allison won four more races in 1992, but lost the Winston Cup championship after crashing in the season's final race.

OPPOSITE: In one of the many trophy photos for which Jeff Gordon posed after winning his Twin 125 qualifying race, he meets Brooke Sealey (left), a Miss Winston, for the first time. It was the first Speedweeks for both of them. They began dating and were married in 1994.
LEFT: Two-time NASCAR Grand National champion Ned Jarrett chats with his son, Dale, in the garage during 1993 Speedweeks. The elder Jarrett, who nearly won the 1963 race, was behind the CBS microphone 30 years later as his son charged to victory.
BELOW: Petty gets the squeeze as he goes three wide through the tri-oval with Ken Schrader (25) below him and Bill Elliott on the outside. Petty started from the pole position and led three times for a total of 19 laps.

1993

THE STAGE WAS SET FOR CONTROVERSY IN 1993 when NASCAR allowed General Motors to make some body modifications during the off season to improve the aerodynamics of the Chevrolet Lumina and Pontiac Grand Prix.

The discontent remained under the surface after Kyle Petty won the pole position in a Pontiac at a lower-then-expected 189.426 mph on an overcast, almost foggy day. Dale Jarrett, driving a Chevrolet, won the second starting spot. Petty had been strong throughout practice and was running better than he ever had at Daytona. Jarrett's speed was unexpected.

The discontent boiled over when Dale Earnhardt pasted the field in the Busch Clash, charging from 13th to first in less than six laps to win in his black Chevrolet. "NASCAR has completely eliminated us from this week," complained defending 500 champion Davey Allison. "It's obvious to me that the Chevrolets did the best job of politicking over the winter."

Ford drivers complained that NASCAR allowed the Chevys and Pontiacs to modify their front and rear ends far too much. They said their Thunderbirds were not as balanced as the GM cars, especially on old tires. GM drivers countered that Ford had already received similar changes. NASCAR's Chip Williams agreed: "All of the cars are very, very close. What it boils down to is we put (the GM cars) on equal ground with the Ford Thunderbirds."

A pair of Chevys won the Twin 125s, but Fords finished second in both races. Jeff Gordon, a 21-year-old rookie who was car owner Rick Hendrick's gamble as the next superstar, won the first race. "Yesssssss! Yesssssss!"' Gordon screamed on his radio as he took the checkered flag. "Oh my God! I can't believe it! Yesssssss!" Gordon needed directions to victory lane.

Dale Earnhardt followed his usual Speedweeks pattern

ABOVE: One of Dale Jarrett's crewmen interrupted a trophy photograph with a cooler of water across Jarrett's chest. Car owner Joe Gibbs, a former NFL coach and veteran of many game-winning baths, was not in the line of fire for this one.

by winning the second qualifier. Earnhardt led the final 24 laps and won by a comfortable 1 1/2 car lengths over Geoff Bodine. Jarrett was third. It was Earnhardt's fourth consecutive Twin 125 victory. Two days later, he made it four straight Goody's 300 victories. Again, Earnhardt was the solid favorite to win the 500.

"I'm, like, waitin' on Santa Claus here," Earnhardt said after the 300. But Earnhardt had proved time and again that a good Speedweeks does not ordain a 500 victory. Others were confident, too. Kyle Petty was hungrier than he'd ever been. He told friends, "I can win this race." Petty's car carried a No. 43 decal with, "Thanks, Dad."

Gordon, meanwhile, fell ill the day after winning his Twin 125. He was in bed by 6 p.m. Friday. "People kept asking me how I was going to handle the success, and I guess I handled it by getting sick," he said.

Gordon was fine by race day, and he passed Petty and Jarrett to lead the first lap. Jarrett quickly returned the favor and led the next five laps. The side-by-side action was incredible as Earnhardt took the lead, then Petty, then Gordon again, then a resurgent Ken Schrader.

Earnhardt kept charging to the front, leading six laps here, 12 laps there. As the race wore on, the suspense grew as the action intensified. On lap 157, Al Unser Jr., making his first Winston Cup start in a Hendrick Chevy, bumped with Earnhardt in the lead pack and then plowed into Bobby Hillin.

Petty slammed on his brakes to avoid Hillin, but Hillin's car veered backward into his path and they collided. Petty's great opportunity was over. Petty came out of his car in a fury and engaged Hillin in a brief shoving and shouting match.

When the race restarted, a different driver led each lap from 164 to 169, as Derrike Cope, Sterling Marlin, Earnhardt and unheralded Hut Stricklin traded the lead. On lap 169, all hell broke loose. Cope and Michael Waltrip collided coming off turn two. They recovered but bumped Rusty Wallace into the backstretch grass. Wallace's car barrel-rolled twice, flipped end over end one-and-a-half times and then barrel-rolled several more times in one of the most spectacular crashes ever seen at Daytona.

Just before the crash, Wallace was feeling great about finally having a good 500. "And then it happened," he recalled later. "I can't remember if I closed my eyes or not. I'm sure I did. But I was with it the whole time. It happened so fast. Bam! Bam! Bam! Bam! Bam! Splat! And then I'm okay." Rusty crawled out with only two cuts under his chin that took six stitches to close. More than anything else, he was angry.

Earnhardt led when the race resumed on lap 174. But Jarrett, who hadn't led since the sixth lap, was directly behind him. Jarrett jumped ahead on lap 177, but Earnhardt passed him on lap 179 to retake the lead. And there Earnhardt stayed for 21 laps, as Jarrett tested him, watching for weaknesses.

Jarrett could go flat out all the way around the track and remain low in the turns. "So I was kind of setting up things to see where I could make a run at him," Jarrett said. "And then I noticed he was starting to get a little bit loose."

On lap 199, Earnhardt's car slid up the banking in turns three and four. Jarrett dove into the gap and the two cars roared under the white flag side by side, with Earnhardt still leading. But as they approached the first turn, Geoff Bodine, one of Earnhardt's bitterest opponents, jumped behind Jarrett's draft and pushed him into the lead. As Jarrett came toward the checkered flag, his father, two-time Winston Cup champion Ned Jarrett, was the CBS color commentator. Producer Bob Stenner told Ned to bring his son to the flag.

"C'mon, Dale," his father said. "Go, baby, go! Don't let him get on the inside coming in the turn!" In the pits, car owner Joe Gibbs, starting only his second Winston Cup season, felt the same thrill he experienced in football. "I'm one of the most fortunate individuals in the world—to win three Super Bowls and now, the Super Bowl of motorsports," Gibbs said afterward.

In the garage, Earnhardt emerged from his car once again a loser. He had led 107 laps. "Big damn deal," he said, "I lost another Daytona 500. We've lost this race about every way you can lose it. We've been outgassed, out-tired, outrun, out-everythinged. We've come close, but we've not won it about every way you can't win it."

LEFT: The wreckage of Rusty Wallace's Miller Ford is hauled back to the garage on a flatbed truck after his flip down the backstretch on lap 169. Wallace walked away with only a cut on his chin. Less than three months later, he tumbled down the frontstretch at Talladega. RIGHT: His best chance at a Daytona 500 victory now gone, pole winner Kyle Petty hops from his car after confronting Bobby Hillin following their collision in the tri-oval on lap 157.

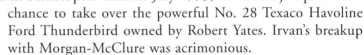

1994

ABOVE: Sterling Marlin watches as two of his crew members work on the engine of the Kodak Chevrolet in the Winston Cup garage. Recalled Marlin: "We'd been like third or fourth fastest in testing. And knowing the history of the 4 car on the superspeedways—I'd run second to it three or four times—I just felt like we had a real good shot to win the race."
RIGHT: After running fourth fastest in qualifications, Sterling Marlin poses in front of his car on pit road for publicity photos. As the 1994 season got underway, Marlin's winless streak extended back 17 seasons.

AS THE 1994 NASCAR WINSTON CUP SEASON STARTED, Sterling Marlin had raced more than any other driver without winning. Marlin had started 278 races since 1976 and never seen victory lane, although he had once celebrated there.

In 1973, when Marlin was 15, he had joined his father, Coo Coo, in Daytona's victory lane after his win in a Twin 125. It was Coo Coo's only victory in 14 years of racing. Sterling had followed in his father's footsteps.

But in 1994, Marlin was the new driver for a Morgan-McClure team determined to win another Daytona 500. Car owners Larry McClure and Tim Morgan and crew chief Tony Glover had been stung in 1993 by the mid-season departure of their star driver, Ernie Irvan. The team and Irvan had grown up together, sharing their first victory in 1990 and winning the 500 in 1991.

After Davey Allison's tragic death in a helicopter crash in July 1993, Irvan had jumped at the chance to take over the powerful No. 28 Texaco Havoline Ford Thunderbird owned by Robert Yates. Irvan's breakup with Morgan-McClure was acrimonious.

Irvan had gone on to win two races for Yates in 1993, while Morgan-McClure sagged. Three different journeymen drivers had failed to post even a top 10. When the season ended, the team channeled its anger and disappointment into an obsession to win again at Daytona.

Despite Marlin's winless streak, McClure and Glover were attracted to the easy-going, likable Tennessean. Marlin was particularly fast on superspeedways. McClure and Glover recruited Marlin on Halloween night in Phoenix after the race there. Recalled Glover: "I had on my Daytona 500 ring and Larry had his on. And we just showed him our rings and told him if he wanted to win the Daytona 500, he needed to come drive for us. From that point on, we were on a mission."

A rookie won the pole for the first time in 500 history when

Loy Allen Jr. turned a lap of 190.158 mph in a Ford Thunderbird. It was a somber first weekend of Speedweeks after Neil Bonnett, veteran of 14 Daytona 500s, lost his life in a single-car accident during the opening hour of practice. Three days later, on a quiet Monday morning, rookie Rodney Orr died in another single-car crash. NASCAR had already moved to enhance safety by ordering roof flaps on cars to prevent them from getting airborne during a spin.

After Bonnett's crash, Dale Earnhardt spoke eloquently about his close friend and hunting companion. "He was the happiest I had seen him in the last three years," Earnhardt said. "You just wonder, why? Why this race? Why this year? But that is the side of racing that is there. I live with it. I understand it. I have no problem with it."

Several drivers spoke during the Twin 125 drivers meeting. "These cars just don't flip by themselves or spin out by themselves," Rusty Wallace said. "I've been upside down at Daytona and I've been upside down at Talladega and I'm telling you, it hurts."

In the first 125, Irvan beat Wallace to the line by .42 seconds. Earnhardt won the second race—his fifth consecutive 125 victory. Marlin finished second. The next day, Earnhardt won another International Race of Champions event. On Saturday, he captured his fifth straight Goody's 300 by passing Terry Labonte on the last lap with a vintage slingshot pass. Afterward, Earnhardt said, "I had a banana split the night before every race this week. I'm not going to change. Would you?" With that, the 42-year-old reigning Winston Cup champion headed to his yacht for banana split number four.

Two days before the 500, fans saw a sight they hadn't seen in 30 years when Goody's Dash driver Dave Stacy tumbled over the earthen berm on the backstretch and with his last rollover plopped into Lake Lloyd. Stacy, who had obtained a fishing card for the lake, waded out unhurt. "This isn't the

ABOVE: The sun sets early in February at Daytona Beach, and as the last light of another day fades into a Speedweeks evening, the teams of Rusty Wallace and Mark Martin are still hard at work on their cars.

kind of splash I wanted to make at Daytona," he said.

Race day dawned warm, and Tony Glover had a strong premonition during his traditional morning walk down pit road. "We were in pit four, we qualified fourth and we're car No. 4," Glover recalled. When he walked past victory lane, Glover said to himself, "Ol' buddy, I'll see you in a little while."

As the race got underway, teams struggled to find the right chassis set-ups. As a result, the race was extremely competitive. It was safe as well. Fourteen drivers traded the lead 33 times. No one led more than 24 laps at a time.

Earnhardt was never much of a factor. His car was loose, particularly at the end. He faded from third to seventh in the last 17 laps. "I've tried 16 times and haven't done it yet, but I'm not going to give up," he said. "The car was just too loose today."

Marlin's chassis was tight and he did not lead until almost 375 miles had been run. Glover never fully corrected the tightness, but Marlin discovered it was only a problem when he was behind another car. Out front, the push disappeared. That knowledge led to Glover's key strategic move, which came during the last pit stop.

With 60 laps to go, the field had just finished green flag pit stops. Marlin was eighth, stuck in traffic. A yellow flag flew for debris. The field pitted. Most cars took tires and fuel. Glover called for gas only. "We only had four laps on the tires," he noted. Marlin left the pits in second, trailing Derrike Cope. The race resumed on lap 147. Two laps later, Marlin breezed past Cope to lead for the first time.

Irvan passed Marlin on lap 158 and led the next 22 circuits. But Irvan's Ford was loose with Marlin on his bumper. When Irvan nearly lost control coming off turn four on lap 180, Marlin squeezed past and took the lead for good. Marlin beat Irvan by .23 seconds to become the fifth driver to make the 500 his first career victory. As Marlin came to victory lane, dozens of rival crewmen slapped his hand. Suddenly his engine died. He was out of gas. There were plenty of volunteers to push him the final few yards.

"I tell you, it was a long time coming," Marlin said in victory lane. "That last lap was a long one. I just told myself that this was a Saturday night short track at Nashville—you're leading, nothin' to it."

BELOW: Eighty laps into the race, six cars tangled in turn three. This image shows four of them. Michael Waltrip is in the 30 car. Ted Musgrave (16) and Jimmy Spencer (27) are side by side as Brett Bodine (26) slides into the scene. The crash sidelined Musgrave, Spencer and Todd Bodine.

1995

TWO DAYS BEFORE DEFENDING 500 CHAMPION STERLING MARLIN arrived in Daytona, he spoke with Sheldon "Runt" Pittman, the engine builder for Marlin's Kodak Chevrolet. The quiet, unassuming Pittman had a passion for building high-powered engines for the Daytona 500, and his powerplants had twice carried the distinctive yellow car to victory lane. For months now, Pittman had been hard at work on something new.

"When you get out there, it's going to sound a little funny, but there ain't nothin' wrong with it," Pittman said. "It got us about two more horsepower."

When Marlin sped through the tri-oval on his first practice lap, heads turned. His car sounded more like an Indy car than a stock car. Marlin recalled, "A buddy of mine said everybody dropped everything and went up on the trucks to see what was out on the racetrack."

The whine came from new exhaust pipes. After they emerged from the headers, the pipes came together under the car, then branched out. It yielded only a tiny boost of horsepower, but that was enough to make Marlin's car a powerhouse—even better than the Lumina he had won with in 1994.

NASCAR inspectors approved Marlin's exhaust, but not the elaborate, driver-controlled hydraulic pump they found on the Bill Davis Pontiac. The pump was designed to lower the rear deck lid for better aerodynamics. NASCAR levied $35,100 in fines. Kyle Petty said, "Most of the drivers are impressed, not mad."

The next day, NASCAR held true to its promise of progressively larger fines for cheating. It hit car owner Junior Johnson with a $45,000 fine—the largest in history—after determining that he had violated NASCAR rules by allowing an insert in the intake manifold to float free. "By not being welded, it allowed more air into the intake," NASCAR spokesman Kevin Triplett said. "That increases horsepower, which increases speed."

Although the new Monte Carlos were fast, Ford driver Dale Jarrett grabbed his first Daytona 500 pole at 193.494 mph. Dale Earnhardt qualified second. Marlin was third fastest.

For the sixth straight year, Earnhardt won his Twin 125 qualifying race, leading 28 of the 50 laps, including the final 15 circuits. Jeff Gordon finished second and said, "Man, I tell you, I couldn't get him loose," Gordon said. "I was all over him." Marlin was even more dominating than Earnhardt in the other qualifying race, leading 44 of the 50 laps before beating Darrell Waltrip by .41 seconds. It was Marlin's first Twin 125 victory.

As usual, Earnhardt's victory made him the favorite. But Gordon looked in *his* crystal ball and said, "Earnhardt is good, but I think that 4 car is going to be the one beat. He's fast, but he's handling good, too." Michael Waltrip, Darrell's younger brother, who had run in seven 500s, said of Marlin, "He pulled the whole draft apart. He was that strong."

Marlin admitted: "We've got one fast hot rod here. I'll put our car up against anybody's." Still, he took no chances with his luck. On his way to the track on race morning in 1994, Marlin had stopped at a Krystal fast-food restaurant. He wanted a burger, but had settled for a couple of sausage-and-egg 'Sunriser' breakfast sandwiches. So on race morning 1995, Marlin again stopped at Krystal and ordered a couple of Sunrisers.

Marlin and his team were also motivated by garage talk. "The crewman of another car, he'd been talking to the 3 camp and they said they had it won, more or less," Marlin revealed after the race. "They told him, 'We ain't going to worry about (the 4 team). They'll make a mistake somewhere.' It kinda built a fire under us."

And throughout a long, gloomy race day that included a one-hour, 44-minute rain delay, Marlin's Kodak Chevrolet was a yellow brick wall that no one could get past. He led 105 of the 200 laps and made it a one-man show most of the afternoon, although Earnhardt got into the mix at the end.

With 38 laps to go, Earnhardt raised the hopes of his faithful fans when he passed Marlin for the lead. Eighteen laps later, Marlin passed Earnhardt and retook the lead as if he could have done it anytime he wanted.

RIGHT: Another tunnel was built at Daytona International Speedway in 1995 with the construction of Daytona USA and its tunnel entrance. The award-winning attraction, located on International Speedway Boulevard just Southwest of the real tunnel, opened in July 1996.

In the pits, new tires had become scarce. NASCAR officials were doling out the precious leftovers from teams that had dropped out. After veteran Dave Marcis dropped out, however, he refused to give up his extras. On lap 187, a yellow flag flew and Earnhardt came in for fresh tires, which were provided by Marcis, who occasionally tested cars for Earnhardt's car owner, Richard Childress.

When Earnhardt pitted, the other leaders stayed on the track, so Earnhardt dropped to 14th. But he knew his only hope to win was on fresh tires. The race restarted with 12 laps remaining and Earnhardt put on another show. He sliced through the field, passing lapped cars and lead-lap cars alike, moving from 14th to second in just eight circuits. When Earnhardt blew by Gordon, Gordon told his crew that Earnhardt had the race in the bag.

After Earnhardt passed Mark Martin on lap 196 to take second, his spotter told him: "Mark says he'll go where you go." But even the assurance of drafting assistance didn't help Earnhardt when he hit Marlin's yellow brick wall. Then Marlin's strong Chevy pulled Earnhardt away from Martin. Earnhardt, on his own, could not mount a challenge. Marlin won by .61 of a second, or several car lengths. "All of 'em are heartbreaking losses if you don't win," Earnhardt said afterward.

"I wish everybody here could sit in that seat and feel the feeling to win this thing," Marlin said. "Coming off (turn) four, knowing you're going to win this thing, and all the people cheering, it sends cold chills all over you."

1996

AS THE 1996 SEASON GOT UNDERWAY, new NASCAR rules reduced speeds by several miles per hour. Groping for any advantage, teams began using radical qualifying setups that made the cars slightly faster, but gave the driver a bone-jarring ride.

After practice, Dale Jarrett observed, "They're really a handful out there right now. The cars are 4 to 5 miles per hour slower than last year, so they should be easier to drive. But the things we do to gain the speed back really make the car not drive good."

Teams used softer springs and modified the shock absorbers to allow the car to ride lower, thus decreasing drag. "But the car moves around a lot more," Jarrett said. "It's up and down and side to side. It's not like it is getting ready to wreck. But we usually have 3.5 inches of shock (absorber) travel in the back. Right now, it's closer to five inches."

Rough ride or not, Jarrett was happy to be driving his No. 88 Ford Quality Care Thunderbird owned by Robert Yates. He had joined Yates in 1995 to fill in for Ernie Irvan, who had a long recovery after a near-fatal crash at Michigan in August 1994. Jarrett had a difficult 1995 season in Irvan's vaunted No. 28 Texaco Havoline Ford, winning only one race. But now Irvan was back in the Texaco Ford, and Jarrett had his own team and his own crew chief, Todd Parrott. Yates felt obligated to both drivers, so he expanded. In doing so, Yates sparked the movement toward multi-car teams.

Dale Earnhardt proved to be most adept with the rough-riding cars, winning his first Daytona 500 pole position at a speed of 189.510 mph. It was a surprise to many that Earnhardt had never won the pole, considering

how thoroughly he had dominated the other preliminary Speedweeks events.

Irvan qualified second, giving his comeback a jump-start. Jarrett was third fastest. The next day, Jarrett won the Busch Clash, leading four Chevrolets across the line. In the final 10-lap segment, Jarrett had mimicked an Earnhardt move and rocketed from the back of the pack to the front in less than a lap.

The highlight of the Twin 125s was Irvan's victory in the second race. It was his first victory since Sears Point in May 1994, and capped a remarkable comeback. Irvan led flag to flag, but on the last lap he had to hold off a double-drafting move by Ken Schrader and Jeff Gordon. Schrader and Irvan went side by side through much of the final lap, but Irvan edged forward at the finish line by about four feet. It was redemption for Irvan, who said, "I wouldn't have been happy if I never got in a race car again."

In the first race, Dale Earnhardt won his seventh straight Twin 125. He led 21 laps and crossed the finish line just ahead of Sterling Marlin. Then he continued his usual Speedweeks schedule by winning the International Race of Champions event. Once again, Earnhardt was the favorite. But his 500 jinx was so powerful, other drivers had to be considered, too, particularly Jarrett and Irvan.

The race was ultracompetitive. By lap 28, Irvan, Schrader, Earnhardt, Terry Labonte and Jarrett had all led. Others were strong, too. John Andretti led twice for 23 laps. Bill Elliott was in front for 29 laps. By the time it was over, 15 drivers had led the race. On lap 77, Sterling Marlin took the lead for the first time in his bid to be the first to win three straight 500s. On lap 80, his engine broke.

The close racing took its toll. Jeff Gordon crashed on lap 14 and took five cars with him, including hard-luck Rusty Wallace, who crashed in the 500 for the sixth straight year. Wallace still managed to finish on the lead lap in 16th. On lap 28, Earnhardt lost an ignition and suddenly slowed. Irvan slowed behind him, but was hit by Wally Dallenbach and careened into the wall. On lap 128, Andretti wrecked. Eight other cars tangled on lap 159.

But with 25 laps to go, the lead pack was still huge, with Earnhardt, Schrader and Jarrett at the front. On lap 177, Jarrett pulled alongside Earnhardt on the backstretch. With help from Dallenbach, Jarrett scooted into the lead. Earnhardt started looking for drafting help from fellow Chevrolet drivers.

Earnhardt radioed his spotter: "Go to Schrader's spotter and tell him he's going to need some help to get by (Jarrett). Tell him to go with us." A lap or so later, Earnhardt's spotter replied that Schrader would help, not knowing that Schrader had already arranged to work with Mark Martin, even though Martin was a rival Ford driver.

The contest became Jarrett's motor versus Earnhardt's guile. But without drafting help, Earnhardt's guile was no match for the Robert Yates engine. On the last lap, Jarrett simply moved back and forth on the backstretch to keep Earnhardt behind him before cruising under the checkered flag for his second Daytona 500 victory. Schrader was third, followed by Martin and Jeff Burton.

And so on his 18th attempt, Earnhardt had found yet another way to lose. This time there was no crash, no handling problems, no blown tire, no last lap pass. This time, he just didn't have the muscle. And he had no help from his none-too-sympathetic fellow drivers.

"Mark was willing to work with us," Schrader said afterward, explaining why he drafted with Martin. "I couldn't have got (Earnhardt) past (Jarrett). I could have maybe helped him, but it was going to cost me more than a couple of positions and I was really more worried about where (I) finished instead of the 3."

"I was going to go with Kenny Schrader," said Martin. "I wanted to see Kenny win. He was *not* going to go with Dale Earnhardt.'"

Jarrett watched it all in his mirror during the last 15 laps. "It felt like it took a minute and a half or two minutes to run every single lap, because you were doing so much just trying to watch and keep him behind." Jarrett said. "I think I'd rather look in the mirror and see anybody but the 3 car."

Earnhardt made some perfunctory comments for television, then expressed his true feelings. "The Fords were too strong, man," he barked. "(NASCAR) give 'em the candy store. We couldn't do nothin'. Couldn't you see that?"

Jarrett, flexing new power and confidence, said Earnhardt lacked only one thing: "What he didn't have was a Robert Yates engine."

1997

THE ONLY SURE THING ABOUT 1997 SPEEDWEEKS was its unpredictability. Time and again, from one day to the next, assumptions and theories proved wrong. At the end of the first practice, Ford Thunderbirds held the seven fastest times. Chevy driver Darrell Waltrip complained, "The Fords have got us by 20 horsepower." Predicted Sterling Marlin, "The Fords will beat us by half a second."

The next day in qualifications, two unlikely Chevrolet drivers qualified first and second. Rookie Mike Skinner, driving Richard Childress' new Lowe's Chevrolet, dodged a trash bag in the third turn and still won the pole at 189.813 mph. Steve Grissom, a struggling fourth-year driver, qualified second.

The next surprise came in the Busch Clash. Jeff Gordon, who was all but missing in qualifying, won easily. Drivers complained that passing was next to impossible. They predicted dire consequences in the Twin 125s. "I'm seeing real good, heads-up drivers making silly moves because it's so hard to pass," said Bobby Hamilton. "It's just weird."

The Twin 125s were almost trouble-free. One minor accident occurred in each race as Dale Jarrett and Dale Earnhardt swept to easy victories. Jarrett's 125 victory was his first. It was Earnhardt's eighth consecutive 125 victory. "If you can get a streak going like this, it's history, and it's history I don't know if anybody else can match or will match," he said.

On race day, nine different drivers led a spine-tingling 500. Skinner, the pole winner, led only the first lap, but completed all 200 to finish 12th. Earnhardt led most of the first quarter of the race, and Gordon took over during the second 125 miles, leading laps 57 through 90.

Mark Martin, who started 11th in his Valvoline Ford, took the lead on lap 94. But as Martin led, Gordon stole the spotlight, not that he wanted to. Gordon had a flat tire on lap 110 and limped to the pits. Back at speed, Gordon found himself in front of the entire field. Except now he was at the tail end of the lead lap, in danger of going a lap down. But Greg Sacks wrecked on lap 122 and the yellow flag allowed Gordon to make up the lap.

Martin led 52 laps—the most of any driver—but his performance was all but forgotten in the ensuing fireworks. Ernie Irvan led for nine laps, but gave way to a resurgent Bill Elliott, who led from lap 155 until 167, when a yellow flag flew for debris. Marlin jumped in front during the ensuing pit stops, but gave way to Irvan on lap 176. Two laps later, Elliott retook the lead.

With 20 laps to go, Elliott was poised for his third 500 victory. It had been 10 years since his last

one. Earnhardt was running second, but the cruel hand of Daytona fate was about to touch him yet again. Earnhardt had taken only two tires on the last pit stop to maintain track position, and his handling was suspect. Gordon had clawed back to third. Irvan was fourth, followed by Jarrett. Terry Labonte lurked in sixth.

On lap 189, Gordon whipped below Earnhardt as the pack sped out of turn two. Gordon never touched Earnhardt, but the move made Earnhardt's car loose. Earnhardt brushed the wall, bounced back and hit Gordon. Gordon managed to recover, but Jarrett hit Earnhardt's car and turned it so quickly, the black Chevrolet flipped into the air. It landed on its roof, gyrated around and flipped back onto its wheels before sliding to a stop in the backstretch grass.

The crash eliminated Earnhardt and both Yates cars from contention. Jarrett spun into the infield. Irvan drove under Earnhardt's flipping car and its spoiler peeled off Irvan's hood. The hood flew into the grandstands and struck two spectators, who suffered minor injuries.

Earnhardt radioed to his crew that he was unhurt and crawled out of his car. But when he reached the ambulance, he looked back and noticed that all four wheels were still on the car. Earnhardt recalled: "I got out of the ambulance and asked the guy inside the car who was hooking it up, 'See if it will crank.' And he cranked it up. I said, 'Get out of there. Give me my car back.' So I drove it back around here and we taped it up." He completed six more laps and finished 31st.

ABOVE: The race's most dramatic moment came with 12 laps to go, when Dale Earnhardt lost control coming off turn two. After striking Dale Jarrett's car, the black Chevy lifted off, peeled the hood off Ernie Irvan's Ford, bounced off its roof and cartwheeled back onto its wheels. Earnhardt got out, but hopped back in and drove to the pits when he discovered the car would still run.

Elliott led as the race restarted on lap 194. But Gordon got a run on him coming through the tri-oval and went below the yellow blend line from pit road to make the pass in the first turn on lap 195.

Said Gordon, "I would have gone down there to the people cooking out in the infield if that was what it took to get by Elliott. That was my last chance. That was the chance to win the Daytona 500 right there. And it paid off."

As Gordon passed Elliott on the low side, Labonte and Ricky Craven went by on the high side. Said Elliott: "I was history. I knew it. I was a sitting duck there at the end. But I think that goes to show you I can still drive a race car."

A lap later, backmarkers tangled in turn four and 12 cars crashed. As the field followed the pace car during the yellow flag, Hendrick Motorsports cars were one, two, three. Hendrick himself was in a fight for his life, battling leukemia at home in Charlotte, so he couldn't hear his drivers chatting on the radio.

"I tell you what. This is going to be the coolest thing ever if we finish one, two, three," Gordon told Labonte with a lap-and–a-half to go.

"Well, we're coming around for the white flag now," Labonte replied. "We're still yellow. We can't go to green, so it's over. Good job."

Gordon thought for a moment, then said, "I guess it is."

At 25, Gordon became the youngest 500 winner. As he rolled toward victory lane, helmet already off his head, Gordon spotted Hendrick Motorsports General Manager Jimmy Johnson talking on a cellular phone. Gordon knew it had to be Hendrick. In one smooth hand-off, without telling Hendrick, Johnson passed the phone to Gordon just before he reached victory lane.

Gordon shouted into the phone: "We won the Daytona 500! This is great! This one is for you! We did it! We did it!"

But Gordon couldn't hear anything over the engine. He turned the car off. Then he heard Hendrick ask, "Who is this?"

"This is JEFF!"

Later, in the press box, Gordon recalled, "He just went nuts. And I could hear the excitement in his home. That was as much a goal as winning the Daytona 500—to put a smile on Rick's face."

BELOW: As Jeff Gordon eased under the checkered flag for his first Daytona 500 victory, crew chief Ray Evernham turns in triumph to Jim Phillips of Motor Racing Network. Evernham guided Gordon to nine more victories in 1997 and their second Winston Cup championship.

1998

IT BEGAN THE MOMENT DALE EARNHARDT came through the tunnel to begin NASCAR's 50th season.

"This is your year," they said.

He'd heard *that* before. But it seemed in 1998 that everyone said it, from NASCAR President Bill France Jr. to the fans outside the garage fence.

The Ford drivers fretted about the new Taurus, which had been approved for competition only after many compromises. But at the end of the first day of practice, the fastest cars consisted of four Chevys, four Fords and two Pontiacs, with Terry Labonte on top in his Kellogg's Chevy.

Nearly everyone expected Terry to win the pole. After qualifying, the name Labonte was indeed first. But it was younger brother Bobby, not Terry, who won the top starting spot with a lap of 192.425 mph in his Interstate Batteries Pontiac. Terry qualified second.

"Man, Terry is going to be mad at me," Bobby said afterward. "I might not be able to go back to the motorhome tonight." It was the first time brothers had shared the front row for the Daytona 500.

Earnhardt, who was fourth fastest, that evening became the first NASCAR driver to race a stock car around Daytona International Speedway at night. He ran 20 laps under the new lights installed to illuminate the Pepsi 400.

"I never thought I'd see a two-and-a-half mile racetrack lit up like that," crew chief Larry McReynolds told Earnhardt on the radio as he raced around the track.

"It's pretty impressive," Earnhardt replied. "I'd like to see a couple of cars out here with me."

The radio transmissions were broadcast to a crowd of some 20,000 fans who came out on a chilly evening to watch for free.

The next day, the Taurus received a boost when Rusty Wallace drove his new Ford to victory in the Bud Shootout (formerly the Busch Clash), snookering Jeff Gordon on a crucial final-lap restart. It was Wallace's first visit to Daytona's victory lane in a Winston Cup car. "There's more sunshine up here or something," he said.

On the main thoroughfare through the garage area, there was room for the transporters of only the top four teams, and in 1998 it seemed strange that Earnhardt's was not among them. He had finished fifth in the 1997 Winston Cup Championship. Jeff Gordon had won 10 races and the title. Earnhardt had won no points races and ended his 15-year streak of at least one victory a season. In

ABOVE: After the ceremonies in Victory Lane, Earnhardt made his way to the suite of NASCAR President Bill France Jr. His victory had come in the 40th annual Daytona 500 and in NASCAR's 50th year. Said France, "I don't see how central casting in Hollywood could have done any better."

fact, on the eve of the Twin 125s, Earnhardt had not won since the previous year's 125. And he had been winless in 59 straight points races—his longest nonwinning stretch since he started his Winston Cup career in 1975.

On the morning of the Twin 125s, Earnhardt woke up with a fever. He felt sick to his stomach as Sterling Marlin won the first race. Earnhardt was still feeling ill as he took the wheel for the second race. Fifty laps later, he led the pack as it thundered under the checkered flag. It was Earnhardt's ninth straight victory in the Twin 125s. Only one other driver, Fireball Roberts, had won as many as three in a row. Earnhardt had won for so many years straight, he couldn't remember how he had lost the last one he didn't win, which was back in 1989.

Earnhardt led from start to finish, riding in front of a pack of challengers who could do nothing with him. "I got through it and didn't throw up anywhere," Earnhardt said. "I was going to drive her whether I was throwing up or not."

But never did a victory streak stand in such stark contrast to a record of futility. Earnhardt had led more laps than any other driver in the Daytona 500s of the 1990s. He had 11 career victories in the Twin 125s, seven victories in the 300, six Bud Shootout wins, two Pepsi 400s—30 Daytona victories in all. But he was 0 for 19 in the 500. It was the only major NASCAR race he had never won.

Earnhardt took heart from John Elway, who had finally won the Super Bowl with the Denver Broncos in 1998. "Everybody saw that look in Elway's eyes," Earnhardt said after the 125s. "Look at *my* eyes. Today, when I drove off into (turn) three on the first lap, my car jumped sideways. Instead of checking up, I drove on through the corner and came out in the lead. I don't know if I'm crazy or determined, but I'm more eager than ever."

The race was fast, clean and all green for the first 125 laps. Earnhardt took the lead for the first time on lap 17 and led 34 of the first 100 circuits. But there were plenty of challengers. Both Labontes led, and Gordon was in front from lap 59 to lap 106.

On lap 123, Earnhardt wrested the lead from Gordon. And as the race entered its final 50 laps, Earnhardt, like Elway, was in control. The second yellow flag flew on lap 174 when John Andretti spun off turn two. Earnhardt and the rest of the leaders pitted. His crew performed a fast two-tire

OPPOSITE: ISC photographers captured this rare and little-known moment from the victory celebrations when Earnhardt celebrated with fans in the grandstands. The fans had gathered below France's suite while Earnhardt was visiting, and he took a few moments to wander out among them.
ABOVE: As fans in the grandstands share his triumph, Dale Earnhardt takes the white and yellow flags together, ensuring his first victory in the Daytona 500 after 20 years of frustration. Behind him, Rick Mast (75) is three laps behind, while Bobby Labonte (18) nips Jeremy Mayfield (12) at the line for second.

stop and he kept the lead. It was a big confidence booster.

As the race resumed, the drivers behind Earnhardt began battling among themselves for the right to challenge the black Chevy. On lap 193, the battle intensified. Bobby Labonte began coming at Earnhardt with breathtaking attacks from the high groove. But Labonte had to deal with Jeremy Mayfield, Gordon and others. They could never get their own fight resolved. As Wallace said, "I think we all had a little something to do with (Earnhardt's victory). We shoved him and shoved him and shoved him, but we couldn't get around him."

Earnhardt was still in front, with the lapped car of Rick Mast between him and Labonte, when a yellow flag flew on lap 199 after Andretti spun again. The final lap should have been a uniform procession to the checkered flag, with Earnhardt leading Labonte, Mayfield, Ken Schrader and Wallace. But Earnhardt tired of waiting. He put his foot in the gas and sped out ahead of the field to get to the finish line sooner. This time, his tire didn't blow. This time, he didn't crash or run out of gas.

For NASCAR's 50th anniversary, Earnhardt had scripted one of the most dramatic victories in racing history, and ended one of sport's greatest jinxes. He had led 107 laps, including the final 61.

"Yesss! Yesss! Yessssss!" Earnhardt hollered on his radio as he took the checkered flag, pumping his fist out the window of his car. "We won! We won! We won!"

Crew chief Larry McReynolds responded, "There's about 150,000 people here who have been waiting 20 years to see that."

"Twenty years. . ." Earnhardt said, almost choking the words out.

On the cooldown lap, he asked his crew, "You all think I ought to take a spin around the Daytona 500 infield?"

"Damn right," said car owner Richard Childress.

As Earnhardt came down pit road, dozens of crewmen—entire crews from some teams—stretched the length of the black asphalt, one by one shaking or slapping his hand. Then he turned into the grass of the tri-oval and spun a couple of donuts, inadvertently creating a pattern that resembled the

BELOW: The winner's slow drive down pit road to Victory Lane is part of the speedway's rich tradition, but never was there quite a procession like Dale Earnhardt's. Scores of crew members from dozens of teams crowded pit road to congratulate the new champion.

famous "3" on the side of his car. As Earnhardt celebrated in victory lane, fans dug chunks of sod out of the earth where his tires had just been.

When Earnhardt finally reached the press box high in the Winston Tower, several dozen of his faithful followers were still gathered in the infield some 200 feet below. They began cheering him, and he responded with salutes. Thus began an interplay between a driver and his fans unlike anything ever seen in NASCAR racing. Earnhardt gazed down on the scene with a smile he could not control.

"That's cool," he said. "They're standing in my tire marks and getting their pictures taken. They're getting grass." He admired his double donut and said, "It's in the shape of a 3. Well, I'm pretty good at writing, ain't I?"

The fans were shouting and waving because they could see him staring down at them. He waved back. A few minutes later, they clasped hands and formed themselves into a "3." Now Earnhardt, McReynolds and Childress all turned and waved. For a few minutes, the fans were at a loss as to what more to do. But as Earnhardt continued to answer questions in the press box, they gathered in a line, dropped to their knees and began bowing.

"That's why NASCAR fans are the greatest fans in the world," said Childress.

Said Earnhardt, "It's just unbelievable that you could win another race and feel more excited than you feel about the last one, but the Daytona 500 tops them all, buddy. It tops all the last 30 races I've won here. It tops them all. It puts the icing on the cake.

"It's eluded us for so many years," he said. "The drama and excitement of it has built over the years. There have been a lot of emotions played out with the letdowns we've had. Running second (four times) hasn't been all that bad. It's been the letdowns of being so dominant and having a flat tire (1990), of being so dominant and running out of gas (1986). We worked so hard to win the Daytona 500.

"So many people were saying. . . this is your year. I felt good about the week, but they were just so adamant about: 'This is your year, this is your year.' Somebody knew something I didn't know, I reckon."

ABOVE: After the salute from the crews on pit road, Earnhardt responded by cutting donuts in the tri oval infield with his car, steering the car with one hand. His handiwork resembled the number on the side of his car. Fans soon flocked to the spot, and some took pieces of turf as souvenirs.

1999

ABOVE: Three-wide racing is
the norm in modern Daytona
Winston Cup competition. In
this image, eventual winner Jeff
Gordon eases ahead of Rusty
Wallace, who has Mark Martin
to his outside. Behind them,
Michael Waltrip is followed by
Dale Earnhardt.

AT THE END OF THE FIRST DAY OF PRACTICE for the 1999 Daytona 500, Rusty Wallace had a knot in his stomach. He had been fastest during the January tests, and now he was even faster. "I've just got to get calm and get away from everybody," Wallace said. "I need to change clothes and go back to the house and have a couple of beers and get back tomorrow (for qualifying) and get the job done."

The next day, Wallace was an early qualifier, and he grabbed the top spot with his best lap yet—194.187 mph. But it wasn't enough. Mike Skinner reached 194.536 mph. Then came a shocker. Rookie Tony Stewart, making the switch from Indy cars, took over at the top with a lap of 194.599 mph. Finally, Winston Cup Champion Jeff Gordon snatched the pole from Stewart with a lap of 195.067 mph. "I didn't think we were going to be able to beat Rusty," Gordon said. "Then Skinner ran that lap and I said, 'Man, nobody is going to beat that.' Then Tony came along and it just kept getting faster and faster."

Stewart was learning fast. "We're going to figure out how to mount a pen and a pad of paper in the car so every time I learn something in the car I can write it down so I won't forget it," he said. Wallace was sixth fastest, but secure in the knowledge that he had a fast car.

Gordon took the lead in the first Twin 125 and dominated until lap 39, when Bobby Labonte used a slower car to help him pass Gordon. Labonte went on to win—his first victory at Daytona. He had finished second in both 1998 Daytona races.

Stewart led the first seven laps of the second race, but out of the pack came the black No. 3 Chevrolet. Defending champion Dale Earnhardt, who had practiced little during the week, eased past Stewart, took the lead and held on through two caution periods to keep his remarkable streak alive. For the 10th straight year, Earnhardt had won his qualifying race.

Said Earnhardt, "The car was just perfect. All week long in practice we just adjusted small amounts and tuned a little bit. We really didn't do a lot of anything. I basically got in the car and said 'OK that feels good.' It wasn't a bit loose, not a push. Lap after lap it was right there."

Earnhardt was ready as usual. Gordon was plenty fast. Stewart, even in his first Winston Cup race, was clearly a contender. "I may be a rookie to Winston Cup racing, but this is my 20th year in racing," Stewart said. "When they drop that green, it's going to be business as usual."

And Wallace? He had experienced a career's worth of trouble at Daytona. Back in 1983, trying to make his second 500, Wallace had tumbled down the backstretch during his Twin 125, ending up with a face full of mud that almost choked him. Wallace crashed in 1984 as well. He crashed in five straight Daytona 500s starting in 1991. He was running a strong race in 1993 when he was hit by another car on lap 169 and tumbled down the backstretch once again. In 1998, competing in his 15th Daytona 500, Wallace finished fifth—his best ever.

On race day, Daytona finally seemed to smile on Wallace. During the first 50 laps, Gordon, Labonte, Skinner and Jarrett traded the lead. But Wallace was right there. On lap 58, he took the lead. And there he stayed, lap after lap, through the first caution period, past the halfway point and up to lap 122, when his teammate, Jeremy Mayfield, took over for two laps. Earnhardt, meanwhile, was missing in action, struggling in mid-pack with a sour engine.

Mayfield was leading on lap 135 when Dale Jarrett was tapped by teammate Kenny Irwin as the field entered the third turn. Jarrett's car hit the apron and catapulted up the banking, flipping as it went. Behind him, 11 more cars crashed, including Mark Martin, Jeff Burton, Steve Park, Terry Labonte and Geoff Bodine. No one was hurt.

With 100 miles to go, Wallace had the car to beat as well as potential drafting help from teammate Mayfield. But Earnhardt was running well again and back in the fray. The yellow flag flew on lap 174 after Bobby Hamilton spun. Most of the field pitted.

Wallace and Mayfield, confident they had enough fuel, stayed out on old tires to keep their track position. Gordon and Earnhardt took four tires and dropped back in the field. Some teams opted for two tires. The range of choices guaranteed a wild scramble once the race resumed.

The green flag came out on lap 179 and Earnhardt and Gordon immediately began their charge. By lap 181, Earnhardt was third, Gordon fifth. On lap 185, they took second and third. Three laps later, Gordon got a run on Earnhardt coming off turn two and passed him for second on the backstretch.

BELOW: After a fast stop from his crew of "Rainbow Warriors," Jeff Gordon accelerates off pit road on his way to his second Daytona 500 victory. Behind him, Mark Martin's crew finishes his stop. "I was having a real difficult time spinning the tires leaving the pits," Gordon said afterwards. "I don't know if we were getting fuel under the left rear tire or what it was, but I wasn't helping them out much in the pits."

Everyone stood in the grandstands as Gordon moved in to challenge Wallace. It was lap 190. The lead pack was still 20 cars deep. Gordon went low to pass Wallace as they roared toward the first turn. It was the same move Gordon had made on Elliott to win in 1997. Wallace moved down to block. Gordon went lower. Now he was completely below the yellow line marking the pit exit lane. But his front bumper was next to Wallace's door.

Just ahead in the pit lane, Ricky Rudd struggled to get his hoodless, damaged car up to some semblance of speed. Wallace had Gordon trapped. If Wallace stayed put, Gordon would have to hit Rudd, or turn back into Wallace. But Wallace knew something Gordon didn't. He knew the pain of a high-speed crash at Daytona. As Wallace said afterward, "I had him pinned down there and I said, 'Man, I'm not gonna try to wreck a bunch of cars.' So I pulled up and he got me."

As Wallace moved up the track, Gordon moved with him. Gordon never lifted, and made the pass. Then Earnhardt passed Wallace, who continued to drop back. Wallace finished eighth.

Gordon led the final 10 laps, followed by Earnhardt, but it was a battle for all 25 miles. Just behind Gordon and Earnhardt, a half-dozen drivers were going two- and three-wide in a constant battle for position. Gordon thought only about Earnhardt. "Trying to keep him behind me was one of the toughest things I've ever had to do in a race car," Gordon said. "He was setting me up every lap. I really thought he was going to get me." But Gordon countered Earnhardt's every move and won by a couple of car lengths.

On the cool-down lap, Earnhardt pulled his black Chevy alongside Gordon's car and lightly tapped it. "He put a donut on it," Gordon said. "He drove into the side of me and just waved. I'm thinking he's saying, 'This car is going into Daytona USA and I'm going to put my mark on it.'" Gordon was now a two-time 500 winner. But Earnhardt, as usual, had left his imprint on the race.

BELOW: It is lap 135, and going into the third turn, Kenny Irwin in the No. 28 Ford has just tapped teammate Dale Jarrett, sending him onto the apron at 190 mph. In this sequence, Jarrett's car begins to spin, then slides up the banking and begins to collect other cars. A dozen cars were involved, but no one was hurt.

2000

AFTER MORE THAN 20 YEARS BEHIND THE WHEEL of a stock car, Dale Jarrett returned to Daytona for 2000 Speedweeks as the NASCAR Winston Cup champion.

The 43-year-old Jarrett had spent years as an also-ran until his career began to take off in 1993 with his first Daytona 500 victory. He became a two-time winner in 1996. Now, beginning his sixth year with car owner Robert Yates, Jarrett was the champion. And he performed like the champ, too, winning the pole at 191.091 mph. Jarrett's new teammate, Ricky Rudd, qualified second.

Jarrett favored NASCAR's new shock absorber rules, which were designed to prevent the cars from running with extremely low back ends. "Now it's back to aerodynamics and horsepower, and I've got the best of both," he said.

The Chevy drivers complained that the new rules left them at a disadvantage. "It sure isn't as even as they said it was going to be," griped Dale Earnhardt. But they couldn't complain too loudly. One of their own, Mike Skinner, was fourth fastest. (The next best Chevy was 16th).

Some demanded immediate changes, but those who were running well wanted no part of that. As Rudd put it, "If all of a sudden you start changing the rules on the eve of the Daytona 500, the guys that did their research the best will be penalized."

Jarrett continued his dominance in the Bud Shootout, edging Jeff Gordon after a side-by-side battle into the final turn. As Jarrett drove toward the checkered flag, four cars tangled behind him. Rudd flipped and spun through the tri-oval on his roof. No one was hurt.

The Twin 125s were a romp for Ford drivers Rudd and Bill Elliott, who led every lap of their races. The only pass for the lead in either race came on the backstretch of the first lap of the first race, when Elliott managed to squeeze past Jarrett, who finished second.

And what of Dale Earnhardt? After 10 straight victories in the Twin 125s, Earnhardt greeted the new decade with an 11th-place finish. It was his worst Twin 125 finish since 1984, when he was 27th. Earnhardt complained, "That's the worst racing I've seen at Daytona in a long time."

One of the key moments in the 2000 Daytona 500, as it turned out, had come in the early morning

hours before the race, when Jarrett's crew completed extensive repairs after he had a near-calamitous collision in the final minutes of the final practice.

Throughout the week, Jarrett avoided joining the big drafting packs during practice with his strong car. It was too risky. As the last minutes wound down in the final "Happy Hour" practice, Jarrett went out to find some traffic to see how one final adjustment would work when he was behind another car.

He was riding in a large pack entering the first turn when someone ahead of him checked up. Jarrett slowed, too. Jeff Gordon, running just behind Jarrett, couldn't slow fast enough. Gordon tapped Jarrett's right rear and spun him off the track. Jarrett was also clipped in the left front by Elliott. His car was not horribly damaged, but it was bad enough. "Maybe that was our bad luck for the week," said a suddenly serious Jarrett. "We haven't had much."

Repairs started immediately and continued into the night. Yates flew three fabricators to Daytona from his Charlotte shop to be ready to work at 5 a.m. race morning. In the age of aerodynamics, it was unacceptable to just bang out the dents. This was precision work. "That's what makes that car fast," Jarrett said.

All week, Jarrett had been regarded as the favorite. Now, the picture was clouded. But Jarrett's team completed their work almost two hours before the race. And when Jarrett led 85 of the first 100 laps, it was obvious that they had done well.

Others were strong, too, including unheralded Johnny Benson and Mark Martin, who led laps 93 through 157. Jeff Gordon was out of it by lap 32 with an oil leak. He finished five laps down in 34th. Earnhardt ran with the leaders for a time but was never a factor and eventually finished 21st.

The lineup was shuffled when John Andretti scraped the wall in turn two and brought out a yellow flag on lap 157. The field poured into the pits. First out was Benson. When the race resumed, Benson tenaciously held the lead, lap after lap. With 15 to go, Benson was still in front, followed by Martin and Jarrett. High above the track, the spotters for the two Ford drivers consulted on lap 185.

OPPOSITE: Fans have a panoramic view from the top row of the Fireball Roberts grandstand on the frontstretch at Daytona. Grandstand seating has increased steadily over the years and now exceeds 165,000.

BELOW: Johnny Benson, leading here in the No. 10 Pontiac, was the dark horse of the 2000 event. He started 27th, but he emerged as a contender during the second half of the race and took the lead on lap 158. Benson stayed there until four laps to go, when Jarrett got past. Benson fell further and further back, finishing 12th.

Jarrett agreed to go with Martin when he pulled out to pass Benson.

The move didn't work on lap 186. When Martin pulled out again on lap 187, Jarrett looked in his rear-view mirror and saw Jeff Burton and Elliott bearing down on him. Jarrett stayed put. Jarrett, Burton and Elliott shot past an angry Martin, who would complain, "I was lied to."

Benson, meanwhile, stubbornly held the lead. The scent of another incredible Daytona 500 upset was in the air. Suddenly, trouble broke out behind him. Michael Waltrip lost control after being bumped and crashed with several other cars, causing a yellow flag.

The race restarted with four laps to go. Benson still led. Jarrett made his move in turn two. Jarrett said afterward, "I knew that he was going to try to block me. I faked high and he went up there. And as soon as I saw him move up the racetrack, I cut my car dead left. I had a run and (Jeff Burton) helped push me by."

Benson was shuffled out of the draft and fell to 12th. And when Jimmy Spencer smacked the wall on lap 198, the contest ended as Jarrett crossed the line to take the yellow flag. Burton finished second.

As Jarrett drove toward victory lane for the third time, he was joining an elite group. The only other drivers with as many as three victories in the Daytona 500 were Cale Yarborough, Bobby Allison and, of course, Richard Petty. And as Jarrett came down pit road, there was Petty himself, with that famous smile, extending his hand in congratulations.

ABOVE: Dale Jarrett leads the field through the tri-oval. Jarrett led 89 laps overall, but only the final four in the second half of the race.
RIGHT: As Dale Jarrett perches himself on the windowsill of his car, he is showered by confetti. "When I got involved in Winston Cup racing, I had the dream that everybody else does of one day being in that Victory Lane and having a Daytona 500 trophy," Jarrett said. "To now have three of them...it was an incredible victory."

2001

"DODGE IS BACK!" proclaimed banners and billboards all over Daytona Beach during 2001 Speedweeks.

It had been 24 years since the manufacturer had won in NASCAR racing. The last time anyone had even run a Dodge in NASCAR was 1985. Now Dodge was back in a big way, with 10 cars in the garage and a huge "Dodge City" exposition next to the speedway.

Petty Enterprises, with Kyle Petty and John Andretti, had switched to Dodge, as well as car owners Bill Davis and new owners Chip Ganassi and Ray Evernham, whose teams were sponsored by the manufacturer. Evernham's veteran driver, Bill Elliott, gave Dodge its first taste of success by winning the Daytona 500 pole—his first in 14 years—at a speed of 183.565 mph in his No. 9 Intrepid.

Stacy Compton, driving another Dodge, inherited the second starting spot with a lap of 182.682 mph when Jerry Nadeau's slightly faster lap was disallowed after his car failed to meet the minimum height requirement in post-qualifying inspection.

NASCAR had devised new rules, including the introduction of a roof air deflector strip, to make the cars punch a larger hole in the air and allow drivers to pass each other more easily. The Bud Shootout showed that the new rules worked. Dale Earnhardt passed Tony Stewart for the lead with three laps to go, but Stewart returned the favor the next time around and held on to win. Afterward, Earnhardt said, "Last year, I made the comment that Bill France Sr. was probably turning over in his grave about that kind of racing. Well, I'd say he'd be jumping up and down this year about this kind of racing."

The intense competition continued in the Twin 125s, which had a record 21 lead changes. [There had been one lead change in the 2000 Twins.] Sterling Marlin passed Dale Earnhardt on the last lap of the first race to give Dodge and car owner Ganassi their first victory. In the second race, Dale Earnhardt Jr. and Mike Skinner were side by side as they roared under the checkered flag. Skinner won by a few inches.

Earnhardt Jr., 26, nicknamed "Little E," had come into his own in 2000 with a remarkable

Winston Cup rookie season, winning races at Texas and Richmond behind the wheel of the Dale Earnhardt Inc. Budweiser Chevrolet. His success had given his father's company a tremendous boost in 2000, as had Steve Park's first career victory at Watkins Glen in the DEI Pennzoil Chevy.

One night about a month before coming to Daytona, a vivid dream awoke Earnhardt Jr. with a start. He said to himself, "I won it on my second try, I won it on my second try." Earnhardt Jr. told the story during Speedweeks, saying, "I stand behind that as if it happened last night."

DEI came to Daytona with a third driver, Michael Waltrip, who was driving the No. 15 NAPA Chevy. Waltrip, 16 years younger than his brother Darrell, had an unmatched record of futility in stock car racing. Although he had won The Winston all-star race at Charlotte in 1996 in the Wood Brothers Ford, Waltrip was winless in all 462 of his Winston Cup points races, which stretched back 16 years. Earnhardt had signed Waltrip during the off-season and told him they were going to win together.

Race day brought perfect weather and an immediate dogfight when the green flag fell. A half-dozen drivers led during the first 50 laps, including Skinner, both Earnhardts and Sterling Marlin. All 43 cars remained in one huge pack until lap 49, when Jeff Purvis smacked the wall and brought out the first yellow flag.

After the race resumed on lap 53, the field gathered back in one huge pack and raced for 104 laps under the green flag. More than 200,000 fans saw some of the most competitive racing ever. The cars were usually two-wide, or three-wide, through the entire pack. No driver could lead more than a few laps at a time. When the final statistics were tallied, 14 different drivers led the race—one short of the record—and traded the lead 48 times.

The two strongest cars were driven by Ward Burton, who led 53 laps (more than anyone else), and Sterling Marlin, who was in front for 39 circuits. But Ken Schrader, Mark Martin and Bobby Labonte took their turn at the front. Waltrip led for the first time on lap 102 for two laps after running well back in the pack most of the first part of the race.

The second yellow flag flew on lap 158 when rookie Kurt Busch crashed. Earnhardt Jr. was leading when the race resumed on lap 163 as fans were treated to an all-DEI show at the front, with the boss thrown in for good measure.

Waltrip edged past Earnhardt Jr. and took the lead on lap 167. Two laps later, Park took the lead. Then Waltrip went back in front. As they crossed the line on lap 171, Waltrip, Earnhardt Jr. and Earnhardt Sr. led the lower line of cars, while Park was on the point in the upper line.

On lap 175, the racing finally became too tight. Robby Gordon bumped Ward Burton's car coming off turn two. Burton lost control and hit Stewart, turning him into the outside wall. Stewart's car became airborne, twirled around, came down on top of Gordon's car, then barrel-rolled twice before shearing off Bobby Labonte's hood as it came back down on its wheels. Stewart was dazed, but not seriously hurt. Nineteen cars crashed, including those driven by Park, Martin and Jeff Gordon. The race was stopped for 16 minutes and 25 seconds to clear the wreckage.

Earnhardt Jr. led the restart on lap 180, but Marlin took over again on lap 182. Earnhardt Sr. led lap 183. The next lap, Waltrip took the lead. And on lap 187, Waltrip solidified his position after Marlin made a run at him on the outside and lost his position in line.

Now Waltrip had two generations of Earnhardts covering his back bumper. Earnhardt Jr. was content to block. Earnhardt Sr. coached his drivers.

"Tell 'em to run low, tell 'em to stay low," Earnhardt said on his radio on lap 194. He repeated the advice on lap 196.

OPPOSITE: Fifteen years of frustration melts in Victory Lane as Michael Waltrip celebrates his first career victory. This was Waltrip's 463rd Winston Cup points race. He won The Winston all-star race in 1996.
BELOW: Led by Dale Earnhardt, the field speeds through the tri-oval during the 43rd Daytona 500, with drivers battling three wide in places. Earnhardt led 17 laps in the 2001 race.

On the last lap, Schrader moved above Earnhardt and Marlin below him as they tried to pass. Earnhardt now was sandwiched between Schrader and Marlin, but he had effectively bottled up the last threat to Waltrip and Earnhardt Jr.

The crash happened in the blink of an eye. Earnhardt's car bobbled, touched the apron and then made a hard right turn back up the track. Schrader hit him in the door and a millisecond later the black Chevrolet went head-on into the outside wall. The sport's greatest champion was gone in an instant. Moments later, his drivers drove under the checkered flag.

Waltrip had the opportunity to celebrate before the somber news about the seriousness of his boss's accident reached victory lane. He joked that 1 for 463 didn't sound that much better than 0 for 462. He gave credit to Earnhardt Jr. for his stalwart blocking. "He dreamed that he won the Daytona 500 man, and he did," Waltrip said. "I just got to beat him to Victory Lane."

By the time Waltrip reached the press box, gloom was descending over the sport. The interview was brief. "I'm just so thankful for everything he's done for me," Waltrip said. "And this is how it all turns out. It doesn't all seem exactly right at this moment for me."

A short time later, NASCAR President Mike Helton made the formal announcement. "We've lost Dale Earnhardt," Helton said. The tragedy spawned an unprecedented outpouring of grief and tribute for the great champion.

"It's going to take time to fill the void," said NASCAR Chairman Bill France Jr., one of Earnhardt's closest friends. "But I'm sure we will. Life has to go on. Curtis Turner was the hard driver in his day. Fireball Roberts. . . Joe Weatherly. Back before World War II, Roy Hall and Lloyd Seay were the Earnhardts of their era. Somebody will come along."

Even so, Earnhardt was one of a kind. His legend was built on more than his seven championships and his 76 Winston Cup victories, more even than his dramatic triumph in the 1998 Daytona 500. It was simply the way he drove. As Waltrip said, "We all loved watching him race his car."

BELOW: The white flag flies and the fateful last lap begins. Michael Waltrip leads, with teammate Dale Earnhardt Jr. serving as a buffer to the rest of the field. Dale Earnhardt is in third, followed by Sterling Marlin.

Epilogue

And so the story continues. One chapter reaches its dramatic climax on a Sunday afternoon in February. Almost immediately, the next begins. "We'll be back," say losers and winner alike, and the preparation soon gets underway, imperceptibly at first, but non-stop come the cold months of December and January.

The trophy is passed, and with it the quest. The struggle to win the sport's ultimate race, first borne by Fireball Roberts, handed down to LeeRoy Yarbrough, and Buddy Baker, and onto Dale Earnhardt, is now carried by the new veterans, like Rusty Wallace and Mark Martin, and even Jeff Burton and Tony Stewart. The youngsters, such as Kevin Harvick and Matt Kenseth, are just beginning their journeys.

They come back each year to Florida, leaving behind the heart of winter to renew this dramatic spectacle of speed. February in Daytona Beach brings a new season of racing. A new Speedweeks. A new Daytona 500.

As with the cycle of seasons, a new chapter is written once each year. Another name goes into the record books. Another winning car, smeared with the streaks of battle, takes the stage at Daytona USA. Another layer of tradition and history is added to the last.

Time marches on, and it is hard to believe that more than 25 years have passed since Pearson and Petty tangled in turn four. To those who saw it, the scene remains as fresh as yesterday. Their children know it only on film, or in books.

The vast scope of a full new century lies ahead of us, awaiting the dramas of the future to be played out, as they will be, year by year, every February, when the drivers, the mechanics, the owners and the multitudes of fans head south to the birthplace of speed for the renewal of the Great American Race.

ABOVE: At 21, William C. France, the chairman of NASCAR and the International Speedway Corp., operates a compactor as he levels the lime-rock base of the track surface during construction of the speedway in July 1958.

Winners of the Daytona 500

1959 – Lee Petty	1974 – Richard Petty	1989 – Darrell Waltrip
1960 – Junior Johnson	1975 – Benny Parsons	1990 – Derrike Cope
1961 – Marvin Panch	1976 – David Pearson	1991 – Ernie Irvan
1962 – Fireball Roberts	1977 – Cale Yarborough	1992 – Davey Allison
1963 – Tiny Lund	1978 – Bobby Allison	1993 – Dale Jarrett
1964 – Richard Petty	1979 – Richard Petty	1994 – Sterling Marlin
1965 – Fred Lorenzen	1980 – Buddy Baker	1995 – Sterling Marlin
1966 – Richard Petty	1981 – Richard Petty	1996 – Dale Jarrett
1967 – Mario Andretti	1982 – Bobby Allison	1997 – Jeff Gordon
1968 – Cale Yarborough	1983 – Cale Yarborough	1998 – Dale Earnhardt
1969 – LeeRoy Yarbrough	1984 – Cale Yarborough	1999 – Jeff Gordon
1970 – Pete Hamilton	1985 – Bill Elliott	2000 – Dale Jarrett
1971 – Richard Petty	1986 – Geoff Bodine	2001 – Michael Waltrip
1972 – A. J. Foyt	1987 – Bill Elliott	
1973 – Richard Petty	1988 – Bobby Allison	

Acknowledgments

All of the photographs in this book come from the International Speedway Corporation Archives. The work of many unnamed photographers is reproduced in this volume, and their tireless efforts and dogged pursuit of great racing photographs must not go unrecognized.

Much of the information has been gleaned from the clip and photo files in the archives, as well as books in its extensive library and the films and television broadcasts of the races, most of which are preserved. The early Daytona 500 telecasts on ABC's *Wide World of Sports* were particularly enlightening.

This book would not have been possible without the dedicated assistance of Buz McKim, the archivist of the ISC Archives. His friendliness and vast personal knowledge about stock car racing history have enhanced this book immeasurably. Thanks to Buz and his wife, Gwen, for their hospitality during my research visits to the archives. Thanks as well to Nancy Kendrick, who contributed in numerous ways, as well as Bill Voreis and Halifax Photo.

At International Speedway Corporation, thanks to Chairman William C. France and the France family, Director of Licensing Mike Brown, Vice President and General Manager of Publications Tom Pokorny and Director of Photography Mike Meadows.

Greg Fielden has always been a helpful resource as well as a friend, and his unparalleled four-volume *Forty Years of Stock Car Racing* is the most important published chronicle of NASCAR races and history during its first four decades. It was an invaluable resource in preparing the text. I also con-

sulted Fielden's *High Speed at Low Tide* and *Forty Plus Four.* All six volumes were published by The Galfield Press from 1988 through 1994.

Fielden, with Peter Golenbock, was also responsible for *The Stock Car Racing Encyclopedia* (MacMillan, 1997), an immensely valuable and thorough statistical record of NASCAR Grand National/Winston Cup racing from 1949 through 1996. The oral histories in Golenbock's *American Zoom* (MacMillan, 1993) and *The Last Lap* (MacMillan USA, 1998) were helpful as well.

Other key books included *Daytona USA* by William Neely (Aztek Corporation, 1979), *Grand National,* The Autobiography of Richard Petty as told to Bill Neely (Henry Regnery Company, 1971), *King Richard I* by Richard Petty with William Neely (MacMillan, 1986), *The Cars of the King* by Tim Bongard and Bill Coulter (Sports Publishing, Inc., 1997), *Cale,* by Cale Yarborough with William Neely (Times Books, 1986), *The Encyclopedia of Auto Racing Greats* by Robert Cutter and Bob Fendell (Prentice-Hall, 1973), and *My Greatest Day in NASCAR* by Bob McCullough (Thomas Dunne Books, 2000).

More information was gleaned from stories during Speedweeks published in the Charlotte *Observer* and the Daytona Beach *News-Journal.* Thanks to Morris Henderson of the Reference Department of the Volusia County Library Center in Daytona Beach for digging out the local articles published when the speedway was first proposed, and to motorsports writer Holly Cain for sharing exclusive reporting from 2001. The NASCAR Winston Cup and the Daytona International Speedway media guides were important resources as well.

I also wish to thank Buddy Baker, Martha Jane Bonkemeyer, Geoff Bodine, David Bull, Derrike Cope, Chris Economaki, Sterling Marlin, Tom Morgan, Richard Petty, Doris Roberts, Rusty Wallace, T. Taylor Warren, Waddell Wilson, Glen Wood, Kim Wood and Leonard Wood, as well as my wife, Ann, and our children, Sara and Jesse.